# WELL!

## REFLECTIONS ON THE LIFE AND CAREER OF JACK BENNY

## Michael Leannah, Editor

Published in the USA by:

BearManor Media
P O Box 71426
Albany, Georgia 31708
www.bearmanormedia.com

ISBN 1-59393-101-8

Printed in the United States of America.
Text and content edited by Datacraft India Pvt. Ltd.
Cover design and photo selection, editing, and layout by Valerie Thompson.
Book design by Datacraft India Pvt. Ltd.

*For Millie and Francis*

# Table of Contents

Foreword

JACK BENNY
in "BIG BROADCAST OF 1937" — A Paramount Picture

*"Jack was probably the greatest thing that ever hit the planet."*

*—Iris Adrian*

# Foreword

Rare is the person whose life is so rich and prolific as to warrant documentation in a biography. For some so honored, one biography isn't enough; several need to be written to cover all of the many and varied angles and aspects of a life well-lived. Jack Benny's life-story has been told in volumes thick and thin, but still people want to write—and read—more about him.

*Well! Reflections on the Life and Career of Jack Benny* is *not* a biography. The writers in this volume zero in on one aspect of Benny's life or career, analyze it, pore over it, offer an opinion of it. Personal memories are explored. Reprints of two obscure magazine pieces written by Benny himself are featured.

Some aspects of Benny's life and career are left untouched. Mary Livingstone's contributions to Benny's radio show are detailed; Rochester's are not. We learn much about Mel Blanc, but Bea Benaderet is overlooked. Seventeen writers (including Benny) collaborated on this project. Had seventeen different writers been chosen to participate, seventeen different topics would likely have been covered. Perhaps a sequel to *Well!* will address the omissions of this volume.

The material within these covers was compiled with the dedicated listener of old-time radio in mind, but we hope the "uninitiated" find interest and enjoyment here too. Perhaps the book will impel them to seek out and learn of Benny's radio, movie, and TV work.

Iris Adrian, whose quote opens this book, performed with Benny, frequently playing the sassy waitress on his radio show. Perhaps, dear reader, by the time you finish the last chapter, you'll come to share her assessment of this national treasure we call Jack Benny.

The writers here have chipped away at a mountain of material and produced a pile of nuggets for your enjoyment. So put "Love in Bloom" on the CD player and hit the repeat button. Then settle in and enjoy the trip back in time and into the life of one truly wonderful human being.

Michael Leannah
Sheboygan, Wisconsin 2007

The wise would get out of Jack's way when he had a radio script in his hand.

# I Remember Jack

## by Frank Bresee

Jack Benny was a guest on my "Golden Days of Radio" program over a half dozen times during the 29 years the program was on the Armed Forces Radio and Television Service. He was also one of the hosts on the twelve-hour KFI 50th Anniversary program I wrote and produced in 1972. On that show, Jack spoke about his early days in vaudeville and his rise in the world of entertainment.

Jack enlisted in the navy during World War I and entertained his mates with his violin playing. During a benefit performance, his solo bombed, so he put down the instrument and started talking and joking. The audience liked what they heard, and a comedian was born.

After the war, Benny plied his comedy on several vaudeville circuits, playing from coast to coast. At the Orpheum Theater in Los Angeles he met and fell in love with the woman who became his wife, Sadye Marks. He courted her at her workplace, the May Company in Los Angeles, a situation frequently worked into his radio and TV shows.

In 1932, at age 38, Benny was a Broadway headliner appearing in the Earl Carroll Vanities. Ed Sullivan, a popular columnist of the day, invited Benny to be a guest on his New York radio show. Jack's first words on radio are well documented: "Ladies and Gentlemen, this is Jack Benny talking. There will be a slight pause while you say, 'Who cares?'" Lots of people cared. Jack soon became the top radio personality on the air. Success notwithstanding, friends and colleagues remembered him more for his kindness and consideration than for his fame and fortune.

Johnny Grant, the honorary mayor of Hollywood, appeared on my show in 2006 with a story to tell about Jack Benny. Johnny first came to Hollywood in the 1940s, looking for a job in radio. He hailed from Lexington, Kentucky, and was a personal friend of the famous tobacco auctioneer F. E. Boone, featured in the Lucky Strike commercials on Jack's show. Benny hired Johnny to do the cigarette announcements for the show.

When Johnny read the commercial ("I've been smoking Luckies for 27 years …") the audience started to giggle. Johnny, you see, was only 23 years old and looked a great deal younger than that. How could he have been smoking Luckies for 27 years? Jack was on NBC at the time, and there were two broadcasts, one for the east and a repeat "live" broadcast later for the west coast. The producer released Johnny Grant from his duties on the second show.

Benny stepped in and said, "Don't fire the kid. Just put him behind a curtain so the audience can't see him." The idea worked, and over the years Johnny Grant announced frequently on Benny's show.

Another story highlighting Jack's thoughtfulness concerns the Pacific Pioneer Broadcasters, a group of over 800 radio and TV individuals who gather six times a year to honor members of the broadcast community. Honorees have included Bob Hope, Edgar Bergen, Jim Jordan (Fibber McGee), Bing Crosby, Rudy Vallee, Art Linkletter, and Chet Lauck and Norris Goff (Lum and Abner).

Jack's manager, Irving Fein, wouldn't allow Jack to be honored because such an event would open the floodgates; everyone would want a piece of Jack Benny. Jack, however, figured out a way to acknowledge the honor bestowed upon him by the Pacific Pioneer Broadcasters. When a friend of his was to receive an award, Jack asked if he could join his friend on the dais. The Pacific Pioneer Broadcasters were therefore able to honor Jack in a satisfactory, though discreet, way.

Jack Benny was one of a kind. It's hard to believe it's been over thirty years since he left us, but he will never be forgotten. His radio shows, television programs, and theatrical motion pictures will be with us forever.

# The Sweetest Music
# This Side of Waukegan

## by Clair Schulz

When someone mentions the subject of music on *The Jack Benny Program*, most people think of the vocals performed by Dennis Day, the singing commercials done by The Sportsmen Quartet, the band numbers of Phil Harris's orchestra, or the theme songs "Love in Bloom" and "Hooray for Hollywood." But truly the sweetest sounds heard on the show were the melodies that came from the dialogue.

In their scripts the writing team of John Tackaberry, Milt Josefsberg, George Balzer, and Sam Perrin (with some later help from Hal Goldman and Al Gordon) created a pattern of metrical speech that became an integral part of the show. By using repetition, catchphrases, pauses, and running gags, the Benny team produced rhythms that didn't necessarily prompt the audience to tap their feet, but did have them rolling in the aisles.

The writers took full advantage of Jack's wonderful sense of timing. After Don Wilson or Phil Harris pulled a corny joke, Benny inserted perfectly-spaced repetitions of their names followed by an insult along the lines of "Don...Don... Moby Dick" or "Phil...Phil...Denatured Boy." The tune stayed the same, only the last part of the lyric changed: the first name was spoken twice, then came the sarcastic cognomen intended to squelch the joker.

Two was also the magic number when Jack invited trouble by hailing a character portrayed by Frank Nelson. Whenever Benny said, "Oh, waiter...waiter," "Floorwalker...floorwalker," "Usher...usher," "Doctor... doctor," or just "Mister...mister," we knew the next word we heard would be a rapacious "YESSS?" delivered with the glee of a vulture about to descend on its prey.

The banter between Benny and Nelson frequently allowed both men to employ one of their pet expressions. Jack posed a "you asked for it" question like "Are these eggs fresh?" or "Do you enjoy aggravating me?" and Frank let him have it with his elated squeal of "Oooh, are they!" or "Oooh, do I!" after which Jack provided counterpoint with an infuriated "Now cut that out!"

The Sportsmen also annoyed the star of the show with commercials that veered from delivering the sponsor's message into silly patter songs. Benny's attempts to stop them took the form of "Wait a minute!" repeated usually four times, ending in a crescendo of frustration that sometimes generated the biggest laugh of the half hour. The routine became so well established that on the January 19, 1947 program, as Jack listened to the quartet over the phone, the audience used their imagination to "hear" the song spin out of control until Benny reached the boiling point.

Another one of Jack's famous exclamations emerged when he was on the receiving end of a tirade. When Don castigated him for his cheapness with a tongue-lashing that began "You are without a doubt the most parsimonious…" or when an auto dealer said that Jack's Maxwell was "without a doubt the oldest, worst, most beat-up piece of junk I have ever seen," we knew it was the storm before the calm that would be culminated by an offended "Well!" delivered with all the finality of a stick hitting a kettle drum.

Jack employed a different tactic when needled by Mary Livingstone. He'd simply repeat the last part of the comment twice in a derisive chorus. Mary's gibes usually focused on his tight-fisted reputation or his age; sometimes she hit both targets with one shot, as on the Thanksgiving show of 1949: "You haven't paid for a turkey since you chipped in with the Pilgrims," to which Benny replied with an echoing: "Chipped in with the Pilgrims, chipped in with the Pilgrims."

Eddie Anderson in his role as Rochester used a line of skepticism, delivered in his characteristic rasp. When Jack told Rochester to check the pockets for dollar bills before sending his suit to the cleaners, or when he suggested that Errol Flynn might star in a movie based on Jack's life, a refrain of four words said what everyone was thinking: "Oh, boss, come now!"

Although Mel Blanc was not a regular cast member, his versatility as "The Man of a Thousand Voices" made him an audience favorite. His entrance as Professor LeBlanc, Benny's long-suffering violin instructor, seldom varied: the scratching of a bow on strings, followed by a metronomic "No, no, no, Monsieur Benny." When his ears and patience could take no more dissonance, he unleashed his expletive of "*Sacrebleu!*" enunciated lyrically and sounding so much like a blessing that Jack's response to the curse was "Thank you."

The litany between Benny and the Mexican character Blanc assumed is still a pleasure to hear.

> JACK: What's your name?
> MEL: Sy.
> JACK: Sy?
> MEL: Si.

Back and forth the two would go in a seesaw rhythm that included similar-sounding *s* words such as *soy* and *sore*. The duet became a trio when Bea Benaderet joined them as Sy's sister Sue who liked to sew.

Whenever Benny walked into a railroad station, it was a downbeat signaling Mel to assume the role of the announcer proclaiming, "Train now leaving on Track 5 for Anaheim, Azusa, and Cucamonga," a triad of cities as euphonious as Atchison, Topeka, and Santa Fe. The variations on this theme seemed endless with the writers occasionally having Mel stop after "Cuc–," giving Jack a line of dialogue, and then letting the other shoe drop with "–amonga." On the Benny program of December 11, 1949, Blanc announced departures in bouncy rhymes: "Train leaving on Track 1 for Baltimore and Washington/It's leaving now so you better run," "Train leaving on Track 3 all the way to Schenectady/Just one stop at Kansas C," and "Train leaving on

Track 2 for Asheville, Nashville, Kalamazoo/Takes on water at Waterloo." Each bit was punctuated with a "shave-and-a-haircut-two-bits" drum riff.

Blanc's ability to vary delivery in his roles as Polly the Parrot or as the bakery clerk in the "Cimarron rolls" routine hit the right note with audiences, and the writers knew he would be right on key in other roles as well. As a boxer named Punchy, Blanc used the peculiarity of sniffing between words to provide a highlight on the May 22, 1949 show. Jack doubts the fighter's claim that he was once a member of Guy Lombardo's band. Punchy replies, "Oh, yes (sniff), yes (sniff sniff), yes I was," perfectly mimicking the schmaltzy coda of the Royal Canadians.

The show's other supporting actors played virtually the same arrangements in every appearance. As the tout, Sheldon Leonard's opening chord was always the same: "Hey, bud, bud." And his response to Jack's course of action was always the definitive "uh-uh." By employing racetrack terms, the writers rode the nag gags through many variations on a theme, occasionally providing a switch by having Jack get the horselaugh such as on the March 23, 1952 show when he declined coffee, even though "it's a sleeper," in favor of tea because "it's in the bag."

Artie Auerbach's Mr. Kitzel had music in his speech if not in his heart right from "Hello, Mr. Benny," which he sang as much as said. Even when he wasn't reciting versions of his "Pickle in the middle and the mustard on top" pitch, or warbling "hoo hoo hoo" as if he were ringing his version of the NBC chimes, the patterns of Auerbach's Jewish dialect had a rhythmic rise and fall that made his banter with Benny sound like a well-orchestrated chorus.

Conversely, Jack's dialogue with the characters assumed by Benny Rubin hit the same note in a composition that might have been titled "Information Pleas." The pattern never varied: Jack would ask three related questions such as "How much weight is Our Fancy carrying?", "What is the name of the jockey?", and "How long is the race going to be?" The answer to each question was the same: "I don't know," delivered in a slur that sounded more like "I dunno." Jack would then explode with a fourth question such as "If you don't know anything about the races, what are you doing behind that desk?" Rubin completed the bit with his reason for being: "I had to get behind something. I lost my pants." It might seem like a long way to go for a punch line and a quick exit, but as long as Rubin got laughs the writers kept playing that old familiar strain.

Another version of the "Three Benny Opera" occurred with some regularity in Jack's battle of words with Dennis Day. Day would offer an overture that teased Benny's curiosity, such as declaring that he was going to have his tonsils removed. After the three queries, "Are your tonsils infected?", "Has your throat been sore?", and "Have you been catching colds?" are answered negatively, Jack irritably demands an explanation, then regrets it when he becomes the recipient of an inanity like: "A doctor friend is coming over and I don't know how else to entertain him."

Jack marched to a different tempo when someone else played the part of the inquirer. Although Bea Benaderet had a recurring role as Gertrude Gearshift (one of the telephone operators who provided off-key intermezzos with cohort Mabel Flapsaddle), she also portrayed nurses and receptionists requesting information from Benny. The series of questions and answers took on a sing-song pattern that often came back to the same refrain. This dialogue from January 21, 1951 is typical of the antiphonal exchanges:

BEA: Your name?
JACK: Jack Benny.
BEA: Your address?
JACK: 366 North Camden Drive.
BEA: Your age?
JACK: 39.
BEA: Your height?
JACK: 5 feet 10½.
BEA: Your weight?
JACK: 155.
BEA: Your age?
JACK: 39.
BEA: Color of hair?
JACK: Brown.
BEA: Color of eyes? Oh, they're blue, aren't they?
JACK: Bluer than the feet of a Sicilian wine presser.
BEA: Complexion?
JACK: Fair.
BEA: Your age?
JACK: 39.
BEA: Your occupation?
JACK: Comedian.
BEA: I thought so.

The Benny team loved words and when they found a tune they liked they found ways to play it on their own hit parade for many weeks. During World War II they introduced Sympathy Soothing Syrup and, not just content with the music of its alliteration, decided to capitalize on the advertising gimmick of reversing the spelling of a product's name. They invented a catchy jingle for "yip-yip yhtapmys" that eventually spread to Ronald and Benita Colman, Jack's neighbors, who also sang its phrases and praises.

The mellifluous sound of Benny's advertising agency, Batten, Barton, Durstine, and Osborn, was too much for the writers to overlook so they built an entire show (November 21, 1948) around Jack's attempts to call the agency, whose name, according to Mary Livingstone, sounded like "a trunk falling downstairs."

On April 24, 1949, the writers again demonstrated that they could satirize Madison Avenue in a lilting way when Jim Backus, as car salesman Plain Bill, promoted an automobile's most distinctive feature, a "dynaflex superflowing unijet turbovasculator which is syncromeshed with a multicoil hydrotension dual vacuum dynamometer." The function of this wondrous accessory? It empties the ashtray. Never ones to waste a good gimmick, the writers had Mary and Rochester sing it again that night and brought it back the following week so Phil Harris could wrestle with the melodic mouthful.

Although Phil's character on the show was that of a tippling boor spouting malapropisms, the lines he spoke frequently evinced the flair of a brash illiterate. He would burst onstage with "O.K., fellows, here's Harris the star,/So tear up your passes and staaay where you are," "So far, folks, this show has smelled,/But Harris is here and I'm jet-propelled," "O.K., folks, you're all in clover,/'Cause Harris is here and this lull is over," and other couplets that he hammered home with a heavy-handed invitation for applause in the form of "Lay it on me!" Sometimes after inserting a pun, he laughed it up and blew his own horn with a non-rhyming but still rhythmic boast, such as "Oh, Harris, many brave hearts are asleep in the deep, but you're awake every minute," or "Oh, Harris, you may not be the star, but without you the show is nothing. Nothing!"

On one show Jack marveled aloud about Phil's hammy behavior by claiming that "If he was half as good as he thinks he is, he'd be twice as good as he is," then wondered further with "What kind of a joke was that?", which underlined one of the unwritten commandments of the writers: sound is sometimes more important than sense.

A notable example of nonsense carrying the day (and the show) occurred on the April 4, 1954 program when Benny, playing a psychiatrist, stated that his name was "William Jackson, Ph.D., B.A., L.L.B., M.A., B.S., M.D." He then proceeded to wrap his lips around the fourteen letters to produce six syllables of gibberish, indicating that his last name was, indeed, Phdballbmabsmd.

Although the writers frequently employed poetic devices (a hillbilly sketch on the November 27, 1949 show was built around the humor in the rhyming of names *Em, Lem, Shem,* and *Clem*), the dialogue itself formed the heart of the symphony that was *The Jack Benny Program.* Much of the humor came simply from the give-and-take in straight line/punch line form, but the Benny team excelled in setting up jokes to match the peerless delivery of the show's star by devising routines in measures of three, four, or five parts. Most of the shows contain instances of this structure; two examples are given here.

On the May 11, 1952 program Jack asked questions from another room while Rochester and his friend Roy cleaned the living room. Jack asked, "Where's my shoe brush?" and Rochester answered, "Right next to your shoes." Then Jack said, "Where's my hairbrush?" Rochester's answer of "Right next to your hair" was the zinger that seemingly ended the number, but the Benny team wasn't done with the tune yet. Jack got the last laugh: "Where's my toothbrush? And don't be funny."

On the first show of the 1952-53 season, Benny, while looking at the labels on his various keys, explained to Rochester the meanings of the abbreviations on each one: WT for wardrobe trunk, DD for desk drawer, and LC for linen closet. Jack then said, "BA," and waited for Rochester's question: "What does that one open?" Jack's answer: "Bank of America." After the laugh and applause, an encore followed with Jack reading, "SM," and Rochester obligingly asking, "What's that?" "Santa Monica branch."

The pattern of building routines in three or more parts of harmonic progression — from Benny's banter with Dennis, to his conversations with Phil, to Mary's letters from her mother — usually reached a climax as emphatic as the clashing of cymbals. The cadence of the dialogue became so ingrained in the actors that they adjusted to bloopers or hesitations without missing a beat. The errors often drew bigger laughs than the original lines ever promised, which demonstrated that even when out of sync the cast played in perfect harmony.

The Benny writers knew a good thing when they wrote it *and* when they heard it, so clinkers (Dreer Poosen, Chiss sweeze, grass reek) at times were reprised. The writers brought back the refrains of running gags ("What happened to the gas man?", "Did you hunt bear?") until they limped. Similarly, songs riding high on the record charts ("Come On-A My House," "Hernando's Hideaway," "Mule Train") were squeezed into the scripts as much as possible.

The musicality of *The Jack Benny Program* is readily apparent when one listens to the parody the Beverly Hills Beavers offered on the April 23, 1950 broadcast. The children's voices (even the growl of the youngster playing Rochester) do not sound very much like the cast members they are impersonating, yet Mary's sassiness, Phil's braggadocio, Dennis's daffiness, and Jack's exasperation come through in well-orchestrated strains of parrying and thrusting. Jack and Mary, who sat in the audience with the radio listeners that night, liked what they heard and could have said what we think whenever we listen to the beloved series: "They're playing our song."

To call the Benny writing team composers and to label Jack and his fellow actors virtuosos would be presumptuous, but just as Big Bands played a unique style of music, the scripts of *The Jack Benny Program* had distinctive patterns tailored to performers whose special delivery made that show sound different from any other on the air. So let the good times roll for the fans of one Benny who snap their fingers to the beat of "Sing, Sing, Sing" *and* for those who favor the other Benny who hold their sides to the rhythm of "Laugh, Laugh, Laugh."

From left to right: Eddie Anderson (Rochester), the Sportsmen Quartet (Bill Days, Max Smith, Marty Sperzel, Gurney Bell), Don Wilson, Phil Harris, Hilliard Marks, Jack Benny, Mary Livingstone, musical director Mahlon Merrick (seated), Dennis Day, actresses Jane Morgan and Gloria Gordon, Mel Blanc.

# In the Movies with Jack Benny

## by Kay Linaker

(From an August 26, 2004 interview transcribed by Janine Marr.)

In *Man About Town* (1939), I played the part of Jack Benny's British secretary. My character worked for Jack when he was in England. I was a guide for him, a Mother Superior-type. I had a good time playing that role.

When the director, Mark Sandrich, cast Benny's next picture he said, "Now for this part I want an American Kay Linaker." An assistant told him, "Kay Linaker's not really British, you know," and Sandrich said, "Oh, yes, she is. She just finished working for me and I want the same type of person."

So the casting director called my agent. When I came on the set, Mark looked at me and said, "You're here under false pretenses. I need an American for this part." I said, "But I am an American." He said, "No, no, no, no—you're British." I told him I was born in Pine Bluff, Arkansas. Very definitely an American. He said, "Go on over to Wardrobe."

So I saw Edith Head, the designer for Paramount and a most talented woman. She liked me because I was easy to fit and I could wear the kind of clothing she liked, which was for tall, slim brunettes.

I was quite tall. This was in a time before the models came out to California and were put under contract. They had to find a place for all of these lovely people, and every once in a while they did a film in which they could use a lot of beautiful girls who were not necessarily actresses, but models. Occasionally some of them did make it in acting—Cobina Wright, Jr. was in *Charlie Chan in Rio* (1941). I was different. I developed a reputation for being a working actress, and for five or six years I was very, very busy.

I did a couple of films for John Ford. Now if you were in a John Ford picture and showed you were easy to get along with and were professional in behavior, you stood a good chance of becoming a member of what was known as the Ford Stock Company. And that meant he found a place for you, no matter what the picture was. I was lucky to find a place in the John Ford Stock Company.

Then came World War II. Having no skills in the song-and-dance department, and not being a stand-up comedian like Martha Raye, I couldn't go on USO tours. But I wanted to make a viable contribution to the war effort, so I joined the American Red Cross. When the Red Cross looked over my application, they found I had a college degree and that I had taken psychology courses. I'd chosen the courses to help me in understanding human nature, with the goal of becoming a better character actor.

They said I belonged in their hospital unit. Now the only drugs they dispensed at that time were sleeping pills. There were no programs for psychiatric patients and a lot of returnees were having problems, so my first assignment at the psychiatric hospital was quite a challenge. When they found out about my "background," which amounted to just a couple of courses in psychology, I was put into the psychiatric department of the Red Cross services.

When they brought in the women who had been at Pearl Harbor, a girl came into our recreation hall. Something set her off, and she started climbing the steam radiator on the wall and was badly burned. After that they put me in charge and we developed a special service to help people with such problems.

I met my husband [Howard Phillips] when I was in the Red Cross. When I got married, I failed to notify the Screen Actors Guild and other unions as to my whereabouts. Kay Linaker went out of existence and Kate Phillips came in. I've never been sorry.

When I was teaching in Canada, I was asked to play a part in a summer theater. Before taking a role, I had to find out what I owed Actors Equity. So I got in touch with the union in Canada and they found that I had not taken an honorable withdrawal when I joined the Red Cross. But since I was one of the first two hundred members of the Screen Actors Guild, dues had been paid to Equity *and* the Screen Actors Guild. Back then, most of us didn't have a sense for legal matters and the red tape that went with it.

When Jack Benny was doing *Man About Town,* he had some problems with the government because he bought some jewelry for Mary—two diamond bracelets, one with emeralds, the other with sapphires—from a man who had smuggled the jewelry into the country. Of course, according to the law, ignorance is no excuse. Jack was in great trouble.

We were in the middle of the picture. I was sitting outside my canvas dressing room when Jack came tearing out of his dressing room. His business manager had just gone in to see him, and I saw Jack running to the telephone.

"But this is not true," he said. "Somebody is out to get me!" He pleaded his case the best he could, then rang off, saying, "I've got to get a hold of my manager. I can't do anything more right now. I've got to go."

We spent the rest of the day working around Jack. For three days he was out of control with himself—he could hardly talk—so we shot around him. Finally, after paying a hefty fine, he returned and got back to work.

I had a wonderful time making *Buck Benny Rides Again.* We filmed on location in the desert outside of Victorville, California. Mary and everybody brought their kids up for a weekend. Roch brought his children, as did Mark Sandrich. It was awfully dull for them, though, because they had to sit still and be quiet on the set.

I felt sorry for the kids so I started playing games with them. We played "Living Statues." I had a portable wind-up record player. They danced and jumped around. When I stopped the music, they had to freeze. Then we guessed who each one was pretending to be, Sophie Tucker or Garbo or whoever. We'd give treats if they fooled us, which they did constantly.

I called Paramount many years later to get some film for one of my students who was doing a picture. She had tried to get a release for some footage, but the cost of it per frame was exorbitant, so I called for her. I spoke to the person in charge of the archives.

"I wonder if I could speak to somebody about getting some film for a student of mine."

"Well, since you have done films at Paramount, I think this comes under the category of previous players not having to pay for footage."

"But how did you know I've done work for Paramount?"

"Once you've known Kay Linaker you never forget the voice."

I was speaking with Mark Sandrich, Jr. and proceeded to have a wonderful conversation. My student got all the film she needed and I had a reunion with one of the truly charming sons of a great director. When Mark Sandrich died of a heart attack at age 44 in 1945, it was a great loss to the motion picture industry. I'm very proud to have worked with him. He was a lovely man; it was impossible not to have a good relationship with him.

Jack had the cast over to his house for a party after *Buck Benny*. Andy Devine and his wife were there, as well as Jack's good friend, George Burns, and his wife, Gracie—she was, by the way, a charming lady and not at all stupid. This was a garden party out by the pool. I've gone to hundreds of parties by swimming pools and don't remember anybody ever going swimming.

Phil Harris and Alice Faye were at the party. They'd just bought a store in Malibu for Phil's parents. Alice was such a darling; she was very nice to his parents. I remember the way everybody enjoyed Roch and his wife and their kids. Such interesting people at that party.

It was Jack's idea to give Rochester the lead role in *Buck Benny Rides Again*. Roch gets the girl and everything. The musical parts were tailored around the person doing the song and dance numbers, and Roch does both of them. By the way, Roch was a damn good dancer. He was the hero of the movie, had all the best lines. Jack provided a wonderful example of a star controlling an entire film from outside the spotlight.

Working with Jack Benny was a family experience; you came to know the other members of the cast intimately. Virginia Dale was just as bouncy as she appeared on the screen. And Ellen Drew was just as reserved and quiet. She didn't quite fit in. She had married a guy who didn't want her working in pictures. He never came on the set, never took part in anything at all. I think he ruined her career. She could have been big.

Public and critical reaction to the film was very positive; everybody thought it was great fun. Jack Benny's acting drew praise, as did Mark Sandrich's direction work.

In Jack Benny's movie roles, romance was always downplayed. Jack was never in a position to put his arms around a girl. If he saw a beautiful girl, he'd make a remark about it, but that was as far as it went. Perhaps Mary had something to do with that. We never saw Mary on the movie set. She appeared only when we were on location in the high desert.

Jack was afraid of horses; he had never willingly been near a horse in his life. When we got ready to do the runaway-horse scene, there was a big rock here, and a smaller rock there, so the pass was just wide enough for one horse to go through. We were lined up so that my horse was first. To one side was Phil's horse, then there was Jack, Jack's horse, and Jack's double, followed by the rest of the cast.

We urged Jack to sit on the horse. He didn't know how to mount it, so he was picked up and put on the horse. The camera was off to one side and high above the action, so during the filming of the establishing shot, the camera got all of us from the horses' necks up. Jack was paralyzed. He just sat there.

We were told to start walking. We were to take a few steps and then let the doubles—Andy Devine's sister-in-law was my double—do the runaway scene. Nobody knew what *exactly* happened next, but Andy said he saw one of the other horses bite my horse. With the call of "Action!" my horse was bitten and it took off, which didn't bother me because I could ride. But all of a sudden the white horse, with Jack on it, raced past me. The hostlers chased and caught the horse and helped Jack down. He was a wreck. Couldn't work for two days.

We did the close-ups on mechanical horses. I had never been on a mechanical horse before. They could be set for walk, trot, canter, gallop, or over-gallop. They were perfect in every detail, all of the tendons and muscles made of rubber. Now I could ride a horse, but those mechanical horses were something else. My God, the activity!

When they went into runaway, no matter how good a horseman you really were, you needed to throw your arms around the neck. It was awful. You could see all the pulleys and things—they weren't covered up. Whatever the director set it for—runaway, or over-gallop, or gallop—all the different pulleys went into action and you were given such a ride, you became so jogged up and so upset, that when it was over you had to be lifted off the horse and placed on a cot to lie and get your breath and hope you wouldn't be sick to your stomach. I was in an earlier Western movie [*Black Aces,* 1937] for which the close-ups were done more simply, using a live horse. Thankfully, in that movie we didn't do any runaways.

Working with Jack was one of my happiest experiences. He was the kindest person I've ever met in my life. He cared about other people's feelings. He always said at the end of a rehearsal, "Well, Mark, are you satisfied?" And Mark Sandrich learned to say, "Yeah, it's fine with me, but how is it with everybody?" because if he didn't, Jack would. The man who audiences knew and loved was the real man. I don't think he had a selfish bone in his body.

Jack worked on his radio show during the filming of *Buck Benny Rides Again.* His radio writers came in every day. We had little tents—they were our dressing rooms on the set—and his writers had one of their own. In between shots, Jack, who was very involved with the writing, consulted with them about the radio show. My dressing room was next to the writers' tent. Jack would come to get powdered down after rehearsing a shot, and he'd sit and chat with the writers. I heard the shows being worked on.

When something was even mildly amusing, Jack fell over laughing. If he wanted something changed, he'd say something positive before nixing the line. "By the way," he'd say, "I think that cue's going to be a little hard to pick up. I think we'd better check the timing on this." It was wonderful to see such a considerate gentleman in action.

When Jack Benny was doing his show, he was the top dog. There was no argument about that. But he never made noises like the typical star. He always took time to make everybody feel at ease. It was amazing.

Once, a tour bus stopped on the street outside Jack's house while he was mowing the lawn. Somebody jumped off the bus and came over to ask for an autograph. Jack graciously complied. He talked to everybody, gave them autographs. When they boarded the bus again, he returned to his lawn mower and continued cutting the grass.

He was like a next door neighbor, a normal guy who picked up his paycheck every week and helped out friends when they had trouble. Working with him was a pleasure and a privilege.

Lobby card from *Buck Benny Rides Again*.
From left to right: Eddie Anderson, Jack Benny, Ellen Drew, Lillian Cornell,
Phil Harris, Kay Linaker, Virginia Dale. From the Kay Linaker collection.

# Finding Himself in the Footlights: Jack Benny in Vaudeville

## by Pam Munter

Mention the name of Jack Benny and his radio and television programs immediately spring to mind. But it was vaudeville that forged both the personal and professional identities of high school dropout Benjamin Kubelsky.

He was given his first violin at the age of six, was a child prodigy at nine, and from then on thought of nothing other than show business—not the concert hall imagined by his parents, but the glamorous vaudeville palaces he frequented at every opportunity. Young Benny often skipped school to attend theater performances, leading to his expulsion after his first semester in high school. His haberdasher father put him to work in his shop, but Benny had inherited no retail genes. Without his father's permission, he began work at the Barrison Theater in Waukegan, playing his fiddle in the pit band. It was to be a life-changing decision, placing him in the company of legends Al Jolson, Sophie Tucker, Eddie Cantor, Fanny Brice, Buster Keaton, the Marx Brothers, and Will Rogers.

### THE VAUDEVILLE WAY OF LIFE

By joining the pit band, Benny became a participant in a national phenomenon. From the mid-1880s to the early 1930s, vaudeville presented variety shows for the masses. During this time, the United States experienced rapid social and economic change, augmented by an influx of immigrants transforming the national character forever. The rapid tempo of the changing acts on the stage seemed to reflect the quickening pace of American society.

A handful of men who owned the circuits controlled the business of vaudeville. Each circuit consisted of a series of theaters. Some were spread out regionally; others were part of a national chain. At the peak—around 1915—over 25,000 performers worked and traveled the vaudeville circuits throughout the United States.

Vaudeville was a highly personal medium. Acts played directly to the audience, instead of using the fourth-wall theatrical approach. Most polished performers could create the illusion that the song or joke was meant for just one person in the audience. And the ease with which the actor appeared to perform helped generate a collective fantasy that anyone with the right mix of talent, practice, and courage could participate.

The audience, however, had the final say on whether or not an act was successful. Singers, musicians, comedians, jugglers, regurgitators, feats of strength, "eccentrics," all knew that if the audience didn't like you, you were out.

The normal performance schedule required two shows a day, though in the beginning as many as twelve shows were featured daily. One's status and salary determined the place on the bill. Opening acts were throwaways, performed while people settled in their seats. Typically, the second act featured a singing duo or comedy team performing in front of the curtain so the stage could be set for the more elaborate presentations to come. There were five acts in the first half and four in the second, with the bigger stars playing in the coveted next-to-closing spot.

Vaudeville was a clear step above burlesque, which featured naked women and bawdy jokes. The vaudeville circuit owners were vigilant in presenting clean acts only. Each theater on the Keith circuit posted this sign backstage:

"Don't say 'slob' or 'son-of-a-gun' or 'hully-gee' on this stage unless you want to be cancelled peremptorily. Do not address anyone in the audience in any manner. If you have not the ability to entertain Mr. Keith's audiences without risk of offending them, do the best you can. Lack of talent will be less open to censure than would be an insult to a patron. If you are in doubt as to the character of your act, consult the local manager before you go on the stage, for if you are guilty of uttering anything sacrilegious or even suggestive, you will be immediately closed and will never again be allowed in a theatre where Mr. Keith is in authority."

The star system emerged in vaudeville, a new concept for our culture, producing a chasm between the small-timers and the headliners. While stars made as much as $5,000 a week, the small-timers considered themselves fortunate if they earned enough for sustenance and the costs of their travel.

Vaudeville created the first group of full-time entertainers, people who lived together in hotels and rooming houses, and who thought about nothing but the business. The seduction and adulation of an audience formed the center of their lives. When they weren't on stage, they wrote, schemed, stole jokes from each other, and critiqued other acts—all while waiting impatiently to get back on the stage again.

In the course of his work in the pit, Jack Benny saw some of the great acts in vaudeville, including the Marx Brothers. Minnie Marx, the boys' mother, was so taken with his playing and speed in learning the complicated arrangements that she wanted to hire him, offering to double his current salary ($7.50 a week) and to pay for transportation and room and board. Mr. and Mrs. Kubelsky, who hoped their son would become a classical violinist, vetoed that idea immediately.

## SALISBURY & KUBELSKY

Benny's nearly two-year run at the Barrison ended in 1911 when the theater abruptly closed. He was approached by the piano player, Cora Salisbury, who asked him to join her act and go on tour. Knowing his family would not view this turn of events favorably, Benny asked Salisbury to dinner. As he paced in the other room, she regaled Mr. and Mrs. Kubelsky with the promises and hopes of a rising career in vaudeville. Jack's father gave him three months, confiding in his wife that he was afraid his young son would fall prey to the painted ladies of the stage. Salisbury herself was not a threat; she was two years older than Benny's mother. In September of 1912, Benny left home, never again to live in Waukegan.

Salisbury and Benny put together a sophisticated act. Dressed in formal attire, they billed themselves "Salisbury and Kubelsky: From Grand Opera to Ragtime" and debuted the act at the Majestic Theater in Gary, Indiana. They were paid $50 a week, with Benny pocketing $15, and were second on the bill. He began the practice of sending money from every paycheck to his Waukegan pal, Julius Synikan, who squirreled it away for him for a rainy day. He continued this for many years and the two men remained lifelong friends.

Opening their act with "The Poet and Peasant Overture," Benny's highlight came later in the show when he played a stirring version of "The Rosary," which inevitably brought tears to the eyes of many in the audience. The duo traveled throughout the Midwest. When they weren't performing their act, they were polishing it. Traveling extensively, vaudeville performers worked the same act for months at a time. Few in the audience noticed (or minded) repetition of material when the act came around again.

"It wasn't easy," Benny recalled later in life. "The whole thing was a grind…We would hit a town, head for the cheapest boardinghouse, locate the theater, make sure we had glossy photos for the management to display outside, then go and unpack." They repeated this ritual with tedious regularity.

Three weeks into the act, well-known violinist Jan Kubelik confronted Benny, threatening a lawsuit if he didn't change his stage name. There wasn't room for both a Kubelik and a Kubelsky in vaudeville. So Ben K. Benny was born.

Doing up to five shows a day, Benny was learning how to reach an audience—but only musically. He had yet to speak a word onstage. During their second year, Salisbury had to leave to take care of her ill mother. Benny soon found another partner—Lyman Woods. Benny called him "a Douglas Fairbanks-type" who miraculously played everything by ear. Benny took top billing and changed his name once again, to Ben K. Bennie.

"Bennie and Woods: From Grand Opera to Ragtime" was basically the same act with Benny now adding a few comic flourishes in pantomime. They played the straight tunes favored by Salisbury, but included some standards of the day: "Waitin' for the Robert E. Lee" and "Twelfth Street Rag," both of which gave Benny a chance to mug and gesticulate. In a short time, they brought in an impressive $350 a week.

After living out of a trunk for several years, in 1917 Bennie and Woods got the break every vaudevillian dreamed about—a booking at the mythical Palace Theater in New York. As before, they were second on the bill, following a monkey act. According to Benny, they were met with complete indifference. They had gotten their big chance and had blown it. *Variety*'s review of the act said, "Two young men, a pianist and violinist, opened with syncopated duet, piano solo medley with the player travestying the long-haired musical type. 'Poor Butterfly' duet exaggeratedly rhapsodized, etc. Both with violins for encore laughs, the pianist though holding the fiddle awkwardly. Pleasing turn for early spot."

In other words, they were "adequate"—the kiss of death in showbiz.

Shortly after the Palace gig, Benny's mother became mortally ill, and he returned home. A short time later, he broke up his act with Woods.

America had entered The Great War and when Benny enlisted in the Navy he was sent to the Great Lakes Naval Station, just five miles south of Waukegan. The sailors put on shows on Sunday nights, and Benny teamed with piano player Zez Confrey. In their first appearance, Benny attempted to replicate his stage success with "The Rosary." To his embarrassment, the sailors booed his over-the-top, saccharine rendition. A friend suggested he put the violin down and start talking. And so he began, "Well, anyway...this morning I was having this argument with Pat O'Brien...about the Irish Navy." He paused and the audience started to chuckle. "You see, I claim the Swiss Navy is bigger than the Irish Navy...but that the Jewish Navy is bigger than both of them put together." The audience roared, and the great comedian got his first taste of laughter on stage. There would be no turning back.

A few weeks later, the wife of his commanding officer organized a show for the Navy Relief Fund and asked Benny and Confrey to participate. They billed themselves as "Kubelsky and Confrey: Fooling Around with Piano and Fiddle." One morning at rehearsal, the director needed someone to read a few lines in a skit. "It was one of those fluky things," Jack later acknowledged. "I guess he figured if I could work my way out of 'The Rosary,' I could certainly deliver a couple of lines of dialogue."

With each rehearsal, his part got bigger. The show toured the Midwest and by the time they reached Chicago, he was a hit. He played his hometown and, not surprisingly, the reviews were glowing: "Benny and Confrey have a neat little act in the vaudeville portion of 'The Great Lakes Revue'...Along with considerable laughable nonsense, they dispense some teasing tunes of a decidedly raggy nature. Benny uses his eyes to such effect in this new act that more than one critic has called him the sailor with the come hither eyes. Some orbs, they are..."

## WORKING ALONE — SOMETIMES

Benny was discharged in November of 1918, but his colleague wasn't. Without an available partner, Jack decided to go it alone. Billing himself "Ben K. Benny: Fiddle Funology," he opened in Springfield, Illinois. He couldn't afford professional writers, so he did the chore himself, copying jokes from humor magazines. He was booked on several circuits simultaneously, holding down the #2 spot, but the audiences, he felt, were hardly enraptured with his ability. He tried changing the name of the act. In one run it was "Ben Benny: Aristocrat of Humor." Then the show became "A Few Minutes with Ben Benny."

Then another problem with his name arose. Vaudeville star Ben Bernie complained that Benny was capitalizing on his name. Benny needed to come up with a new one, and fast. Jack and his good friend Benny Rubin came upon a group of sailors who called everyone Jack. Rubin said, "That's your name." Benny replied, "Jack Benny. I like it. Jack Benny."

His first big review as a solo act appeared in *Variety* in January of 1921, marred by Sime Silverman's comparison of Benny with Bernie. "Jack Benny has a violin and talk. Mainly talk. He handles himself as though having played small time, though his talk material is new…His violin playing is negligible for results. He holds the instrument in the regular way under the neck, whereas Bernie holds it carelessly." As critics are wont to do, Silverman offered the comedian advice: "The answer seems to be for Benny to throw away his violin while Bernie is using one, and try another method of working in his talk, if he doesn't care to become a monologist outright…"

Benny took the advice to heart, though he felt emotionally dependent on his fiddle. He later noted, "I was booked to play at Keith's Syracuse, where I had always been a riot. I decided that was the place to experiment and go on without my fiddle. The first day I walked on stage empty-handed, I literally forced myself to go on. I did 14 minutes without the violin and came off soaked with perspiration from head to toe. I was a nervous wreck. The next day, I did my routine with the fiddle again." But a short while later, a fellow performer bet that he couldn't do his act without the violin so, of course, he did. This time the more seasoned performer felt less uncomfortable. After that, he brought his fiddle with him only when he intended to use it.

Longtime friend George Burns remembered Benny doing stingy jokes during this period. The humor worked because of the incongruity. "If there was ever anybody who didn't look stingy, it was Jack. He was so immaculate…so elegant on stage. When he told a stingy joke, the contrast was just ridiculous." At this time also, Benny began incorporating vanity and self-mockery into his humor.

Though Benny had been playing vaudeville dates since 1910, he was still not a headliner. Life was hard and the payoffs few, but, as historian Robert C. Toll wrote, "In the magic glow of the footlights, in the warmth of an enthusiastic audience, an ordinary performer would be lifted, at least for that moment, to exhilarating heights." That intermittent reinforcement—that once-in-a-while peak experience—kept small-timers in the business.

Benny continued honing his act and tinkering with its name. He settled on "A Few Minutes with Jack Benny." His manager and producer, Irving Fein, wondered if the frequent name changes alone didn't account for Benny's well-known insecurity.

As he perfected his routine, Benny was given more time on stage. He believed that the most important moment for him was his opening line. In one of his first solo acts, he stood behind the curtain, loudly playing scales. When it opened, he turned with mock surprise to the audience and said, "Oh, I guess I'm on." Another time, he walked to the center of the stage, leaned over the footlights and asked the orchestra leader, "How's the show going up 'til now?" When the leader responded, "Fine," Benny retorted, "Well, I'll fix that." These opening lines lightened the tone and readied the audience for his style of comedy.

Vaudeville comedians were notorious for being raucous and obvious in their humor. Benny, on the other hand, became more subtle as he progressed in his craft. He stopped telling jokes altogether and began relating stories and making comments, a practice done only by specialty acts like Will Rogers.

Benny tried other devices to capture audience attention. Leo Feist, a music publisher in Chicago, offered him a free singer if the vocalist were allowed a song or two of his own in the act. Knowing a good thing when he saw it, Benny brought Ned Miller aboard for the encore spot. Benny told the audience that his kid brother was backstage and he might be persuaded to come out and sing a song. Miller entered wearing knickers and a hat. Benny quickly removed the hat and stepped aside. As Miller sang, he created the impression that he might not be able to hit the inevitable high note at the end of the song. As he approached that fateful final note, Benny rushed over to him and handed him his hat. The "kid" grabbed it with both hands as if it were a totem and magically hit the note. It never failed to stop the show. Later, Benny put Miller in a theater box using the same ruse. Ned Miller became a lifelong friend and occasional employee—one of an ever-growing list of people able to say that.

## SADYE, SADYE

That list included Sadye Marks, who became Benny's wife in 1927. He'd been playing in theatrical shows and was performing in a Shubert Bros. production, *Great Temptations*, featuring Arthur Treacher and Jay C. Flippen. When the show ended, he signed another long contract to return to vaudeville. He could now afford writers and no longer created his own material. Known as a bit of a Lothario on the circuit, Benny engaged in a long relationship with performer Mary Kelly, then in another with Nora Bayes. He met Sadye Marks through his old pal, Zeppo Marx, a distant cousin of Sadye. After the marriage, she traveled with him from town to town. He put her in the act to give her something to do.

Years later, Mary Livingstone wrote, "Without so much as batting an eyelash, I said sure. I was at that brash stage in life. I thought I could do anything—and I did—going on stage without any previous experience." Irving Fein added, "By the time they had toured for a season, Sadye was getting big laughs on her lines and enthusiastic applause for the two songs she did every show, and she blossomed out as a full-fledged vaudeville performer."

After their first year on the road, they arrived in Los Angeles to play the Orpheum. To give Sadye a break, Benny tried a different partner, but she bombed. The producers insisted on Sadye's return. The act was held over, an unprecedented occurrence on the Orpheum circuit.

Now, after so many years on the boards, he was finally in the next-to-closing spot, though he wasn't considered a star yet. But Benny was developing the formula that would bring him tremendous success. "People like to be panned," he once said. "You can't praise anything and be funny. If you want the laughs, you have to put something or somebody in a ridiculous light, even yourself." His stage persona was coming together at last.

He began functioning as a master of ceremonies at both private and public gatherings, refining his fledgling character. New York critic Larry Lawrence extolled, "An actor who can carry the difficult role of being master of ceremonies at a vaudeville show and not turn into an utter ass and bore the audience has again been discovered. He is Jack Benny, and you may listen to his drolleries any time this week."

Benny was signed to a six-month contract with MGM at $750 a week, making him "Filmland's first on-screen emcee." He appeared in short films and in *The Hollywood Revue of 1929.* The big studios weren't known for their creativity in casting and Benny languished, finding few additional opportunities for work.

Famed showman Earl Carroll was preparing a new edition of his *Vanities* and called Benny's agent. Carroll wanted Benny in a featured role and was willing to pay him $1500 a week. MGM's Irving Thalberg agreed to release Benny from his contract because of the dearth of appropriate studio projects. Benny returned to films later, under much different circumstances.

Carroll's shows were known for their risqué qualities, and Benny took pride in working clean. "I refused to play in the dirty skits and spent more than a few sleepless nights waiting to be fired. But he gave in...I was allowed to do my regular monologue in the second half of the show." Shortly after opening, the theater was raided and Carroll was arrested. Not Benny. "The Grand Jury didn't indict them but the raid, the charges, and the countercharges gave [the show] the kind of publicity money can't buy. We ran 247 performances—longer than any previous 'Vanities.' It was SRO every night."

After the *Vanities* closed, Benny was left with few options. By 1931, much of vaudeville's audience had flocked to the new talking pictures and the prevailing buzz was about the fairly new medium of radio. Benny listened and was surprised to hear names he had never heard before—people who were suddenly national stars.

Benny first appeared on radio as a guest on the hot new Ed Sullivan radio show. The reaction to the Sullivan interview was more than positive, so Benny decided to forge a career in radio. *Vanities* was about to go on the road. Once again he had to make a major career decision. He asked for his release from Carroll and threw his lot in with the fledgling medium. Within two years, he was a major radio star.

## THE LEGACY OF VAUDEVILLE

Throughout the remainder of his career, Benny incorporated much of what he learned on the vaudeville stage into his radio, movie, and TV work. He mastered the art of characterization, knowing that in showbiz it's the personality that reaches the audience, not merely the talent. He developed a storehouse of techniques and tricks that several generations came to identify with Jack Benny. Many of his shows and specials were couched in the old variety-style format—a singer, a guest star, skits—predictable and comfortable for the audience.

Though he didn't enjoy reminiscing, his heart remained tender to the memories of his years in vaudeville. Later in his life when he traveled to the towns in which he had performed, he had perfect recall of the vaudeville houses, remembered exactly where he had stayed, and how the audience reacted to his show.

He made many close friends in vaudeville, such as Eddie Cantor, the Marx Brothers, Fanny Brice, and George Burns.

The symbolic end of vaudeville came in 1932 when the Palace in New York closed and became a movie theater. Vaudeville hadn't changed, but the public's taste and sophistication had. Many vaudeville performers signed movie contracts and filmed their acts, essentially destroying them.

But if movies were bad for vaudeville, radio was worse. The country was mired in The Great Depression. Radio was free and it came right into people's homes. The intimacy that Benny had created in his vaudeville act transferred naturally to this new living room medium. Though he went to school in vaudeville, it was in radio that he achieved the star status that had eluded him for so long.

At the time of his death in 1974, Jack was slated to play one of the leads in *The Sunshine Boys*, a movie based on the vaudeville team of Smith and Dale. He would have appreciated the irony of a life that had come full circle.

Magazine cover, 1949

# The Women in Benny's Life: An Examination of Jack's Luck With the Fairer Sex in Radio, TV, and the Movies

### by Mark Higgins

I'd like to address all of the men reading this book. You know who you are— we who have grown up living vicariously through radio, movies, and TV. We who firmly wanted to believe (depending on your generation) that Wallace Beery could be married to Jean Harlow, that Walter Matthau could end up with Sophia Loren and Jack Lemmon with Ann-Margret, that Lyle Lovett could make a play for Julia Roberts. If they could do it, certainly we, too, had a shot.

At first blush it may come as a surprise, but one of our heroes could certainly be Jack Benny. Sure, his radio persona presented him as the eternal bachelor, forever 39, balding, cheap, with a regular girlfriend named Gladys Zybysko, occasionally dating one of the switchboard girls, Gertrude Gearshift and Mabel Flapsaddle, and regularly striking out with Mary Livingstone, his mate in real life. How many of us, however, can brag of having spent time with the likes of Ann Sheridan, Carole Lombard, Dorothy Lamour, Ida Lupino, Joan Bennett, Barbara Stanwyck, Jayne Mansfield, Marilyn Monroe—and that's to name just a few. Throughout his career, Jack crossed paths with every glamour queen and sex symbol of at least three generations of fans, and the legend lives on today (although much of the legend was probably written by Jack).

Most of Jack's radio and television conquests came in the form of dream sequences, but every so often we actually caught a glimpse of Jack's charm with the ladies, such as in the violin duets with Gisele MacKenzie and the banter that accompanied them.

In this examination of Jack's history with the ladies, we'll look at his various personae, as well as his performances in movies, radio, and television. Over a career that spanned more than forty years he displayed a number of different sides.

## MOVIES

On film, Jack excelled at playing the self-centered egotist easily swayed by the flattery of a beautiful woman. A good example of this was in Ernst Lubitsch's wartime masterpiece, *To Be or Not to Be*. (Jack's co-star, Carole Lombard, was killed in a plane crash a month after filming ended, and before the movie's release.)

Jack played Joseph Tura, the famous Polish Shakespearean actor, married to Maria (Lombard), who is also his leading lady. While it is obvious that she loves her husband, she also enjoys the attention of her adoring male fans. When she attracts the attention of a Polish flyer who attends the performance of *Hamlet* every night just to see her, Tura becomes suspicious and jealous. When the flyer sends flowers to her dressing room, he confronts her.

> JACK: But, darling, you know how I feel about you…why, I'd even…Oh, flowers, eh?
> CAROLE: Aren't they beautiful?
> JACK: Don't be casual. Who sent them?
> CAROLE: I don't know. There wasn't any card.
> JACK: No card again? That's three nights in succession—who is he?
> CAROLE: I'm sure this has nothing to do with me personally. This man is probably a lover of the theatre, an art fanatic, someone sitting up in the gallery night after night…
> JACK: Oh, just one of those poor boys who hasn't the price of a ticket, but inherited a lot of flowers and is trying to get rid of them. Three nights in a row—even Shakespeare couldn't stand seeing *Hamlet* three nights in succession.
> CAROLE: You forget…you're playing Hamlet.
> JACK: Oh, that's right.

Subject successfully changed—case closed.

Later, when Maria works out an arrangement to see the flyer backstage ("Come back to my dressing room when Hamlet goes into his soliloquy 'To Be or Not to Be…'"), Joseph returns to the dressing room between acts, totally deflated.

> JACK: It happened, what every actor dreads.
> CAROLE: What, darling, what?
> JACK: Someone walked out on me.
> CAROLE: Oh.
> JACK: Tell me, Maria, am I losing my grip?
> CAROLE: Oh, of course not, darling. I'm so sorry.
> JACK: But he walked out on me.
> CAROLE: Maybe he didn't feel well, maybe he had to leave, maybe he had a sudden heart attack.
> JACK: I hope so.
> CAROLE: If he had stayed, he might have died.
> JACK: Maybe he's dead already. Oh darling, you're so comforting.

Again, she plays to his ego to distract and reassure at the same time.

At the other end of his movie career, at the age of 73, Jack's lifelong pursuit of the fairer sex was recognized when he was called upon as a "technical advisor" in the movie *A Guide for the Married Man*, in which Robert Morse teaches Walter Matthau the art of philandering through a series of vignettes. Jack's character, Ollie ("Sweet Lips") is featured in the sequence on how to break up with one woman while a new girlfriend waits in the car outside. In a memorable scene featuring his cheapskate persona, he rummages through his soon-to-be-ex-girlfriend's apartment like an auction house appraiser, examining her things while extolling the virtues of a more sensible coat and a steady job. Only Jack could have handled this role with such mastery.

## RADIO

Jack's radio character is the one we most remember, a cheap bachelor with a series of questionable conquests, and only one relatively long-term relationship.

In 1938, Jack dated Barbara Whitney. In the episode from November 20, Jack is on the phone with Barbara, while Phil and Mary are in the next room, eavesdropping.

> JACK: Yes, Barbara, yeah…Oh, you don't really mean that. You do? Uh huh…uh huh huh…uh huh huh huh…gee, that's cute.
> PHIL: What a sap.
> MARY: Oh, let him alone. He's only young twice.
> JACK: Oh, you know I do, Barbara. I called you four times today, didn't I? That's four nickels. That's twenty cents.
> MARY: What a Romeo. He keeps books, yet.
> JACK: Now look, honey. Am I going to see you tonight? Oh, you're going to cooking school tonight. Well, that's encouraging. How about Monday night? I see. Well, Tuesday night? Wednesday night?
> PHIL: When you get to Friday, it's me.
> JACK: What's that, Barbara? Oh, you can see me Thursday night? Well, that's swell. Can I bring you some more peanut brittle? I'll bring you a great big bag.
> MARY: Gee. He must get it wholesale.

Peanut brittle—the way to a woman's heart.

Gladys Zybysko was Jack's steadiest relationship. She first appeared on New Year's Eve, 1939. She disappoints Jack (she called him "Speedy") by backing out on their date. Jack's concern: "But, Gladys, I have two tickets for dinner—I'll be so stuffed I won't be able to move." Dejected, Jack turns down his cast members' invitations to go out with them. On his way home, he stops at Ginsburg's Hanging Garden Restaurant for a cup of coffee. Jack is dressed in formal wear meant for a big night on the town. Ginsburg tells Jack that usually, when anyone comes into the restaurant wearing a tuxedo, he charges 5 cents extra for the coffee, "but with that tuxedo, let it go." The waitress comes to take Jack's order.

> JACK: Oh, hello.
> WAITRESS: Hello.
> JACK: Coffee, please.
> WAITRESS: Would you like a sandwich or some toast with it?
> JACK: No, thanks. Just coffee.
> WAITRESS: Want a little cream with it?
> JACK: Nope, just some black coffee.
> WAITRESS: Gee, I'm sorry about this.

JACK: That's all right, Gladys...That's all right. Forget it.

WAITRESS/GLADYS: But honest, Jack, Mamie promised she'd work for me tonight.

JACK: Mamie. All the time it's Mamie. You could have let me know before the last minute.

GLADYS: I'm sorry, Speedy.

JACK: I see you're wearing my corsage on that uniform, yet. Forget about the coffee. I'm going home.

GLADYS: I'll be through at 3 o'clock.

JACK (angry): At 3 o'clock, I'll be snoring. Goodbye.

GLADYS: Well, if that's the way you feel about it, here's your golf ball back.

(For Christmas, Jack gave her—and everyone else—a golf ball.)

JACK: Keep it.

By January, Gladys is calling Jack "Sporty," and Jack is defending Gladys as a "one-man woman" to Don Wilson.

DON: Well, perhaps I shouldn't say this, Jack, but I dropped into Ginsburg's Restaurant the other day, and when Gladys brought me my sandwich, she winked at me.

JACK: Gladys winked at you?

DON: Absolutely.

JACK: With her right eye, or left eye?

DON: Her left eye.

JACK: Well, that's the one that twitches. That's nerves, Don, not romance!

By his birthday in 1942, Jack's playing the field again, trying to find a date in his little red book. He tries Scheherazade Krump and Thelma Skronik. He then calls on Ginger Rogers...and asks for Miss McGuire. When he's told she doesn't work there anymore, his response is "Well, I can scratch Ginger Rogers's name out of my book."

In 1948, Jack was again with Gladys. By this time she had changed professions. In the February 29, 1948 episode, Jack invites her to the Sunday morning rehearsal of the show. They take the bus.

JACK: Gosh, Gladys, it sure is a long bus ride from your house, isn't it?

GLADYS: It sure is, Speedy.

JACK: The bus has been so crowded, I'm sorry you had to stand the whole way.

GLADYS: Oh, that's all right. Look how long you had to stand before you found a seat.

JACK: Yeah.

GLADYS: It was smart of you telling that old lady that it was Crenshaw Boulevard when it was only Vermont.

JACK: Yeah. Oh, well, the walk will do her good. You know, Gladys, you're the first one I've ever invited to my rehearsal. I wanted you to see how a big star operates.

GLADYS: You mean Phil Harris will be there?

JACK: Gladys, when I said a star, I meant that...

GLADYS: Speedy, I was only kidding. Stop pouting.

JACK: Well, I'm the star of the show, not Phil Harris. You hurt my feelings.

GLADYS: Oh, I know how it is, Speedy. Everyone likes to think they're the tops in their profession.

JACK: Certainly. How would you feel if I said that any plumber can solder a steam pipe as fast as you can?

(It's early, so they stop at the drugstore for a sandwich. Dennis Day comes in, and Jack introduces him to Gladys.)

JACK: Dennis, this is Gladys Zybysko.

DENNIS: Haven't we met before? Your legs look familiar.

JACK: Dennis, if you've met before, how come all you remember is her legs?

DENNIS: That's all I could see. She was fixing a pipe under our kitchen sink.

(Their lunch arrives, and Gladys notices a button in her soup.)

JACK: Hey, waiter, there's a button in this soup.

WAITER (Mel Blanc): What do you want for 15 cents, a zipper?

JACK: No, I don't want a zipper, and I demand to know why there's a button in this soup.

GLADYS: Oh, Speedy, don't argue with him. I just won't pay for my soup.

JACK: No, no, Gladys, this is on me. *I* won't pay for it.

Gertrude and Mabel, the telephone operators, were occasional double dates for Jack and a friend. On the program of March 20, 1949, Van Johnson was Jack's guest. Jack asks Van why all the girls are crazy about him.

> VAN: You know, that's a mistaken idea, Jack. Everyone thinks the girls are just nuts about me and it isn't true at all.
>
> JACK: It isn't?
>
> VAN: No. Confidentially, Jack, most of the glamour girls in Hollywood won't even spit at me.
>
> JACK: That's funny, they do at me.

Jack offers to help Van with his technique. He's taking his girlfriend to Ciro's and asks her to bring a friend for Van. The girls are to meet them in front of Ciro's at 8 o'clock.

> MABEL: Say, Gertrude.
>
> GERTRUDE: What is it, Mabel?

MABEL: Are you sure he's bringing Van Johnson for me?

GERTRUDE: Yeah, and you can have him. As far as I'm concerned, I'd just as soon go out with men like Jack Benny.

MABEL: Why?

GERTRUDE: 'Cause when a man like Benny tries to kiss you, and you tell him to stop, and he stops, you don't feel so disappointed.

Jack and Van arrive.

VAN: Jack, do you think that the girls will keep the date with us?

JACK: Certainly. I told them to meet us right out in front of...hey, hey, there they are now.

VAN: Where?

JACK: Right there, see those two.

VAN: (Screams)

JACK: Van, come back here...Van, what's the matter with you?

VAN: I wouldn't go into Ciro's with them.

JACK: Why not?

VAN: One of them is old enough to be my mother.

JACK: Which one?

VAN: The one that looks like my father.

JACK: Look, Van, that's my girl. You've got the cute short one.

VAN: Oh, you mean the short one with the red dress? She hasn't got a bad shape.

JACK: That's the fire plug. The girls are over there sitting on the curb.

VAN: Jack, let's call this thing off. I don't want to go into Ciro's with those two dames.

JACK: But, Van, these girls are all right. In case anyone picks a fight with us, the tall one can whip her weight in wildcats.

(The dinner is a disaster. After two martinis, Jack asks Van if he'd like another drink.)

VAN: Yeah, but I'd like something stronger this time.

JACK: How about a Zombie?

VAN: No, thanks. The two we brought with us are enough.

Suddenly, the lady plumber doesn't look so bad after all.

## TELEVISION

On TV, Jack successfully used the dream sequence, as in this memorable scene with Marilyn Monroe. Jack is returning from a trip to Hawaii on the ocean liner *Lurilene*, and falls asleep in a deck chair next to a heavyset blonde. Next thing you know, she's Marilyn.

JACK: Marilyn, why did you walk away from me? Why did you want to leave me?

MARILYN: Because I can't trust myself with you.

JACK: What?

MARILYN: You're so strong, and I'm so weak. When you look at me with those big, blue eyes, I just...I just...

JACK: I understand.

MARILYN: I thought all I wanted was money and diamonds, but now for the first time, I realize that all I want is you.

JACK: Marilyn.

NARRATOR (Paul Frees): Dream on, Mr. Benny. Dream on.

JACK: Marilyn, Marilyn...I'm mad about you.

MARILYN: I'm mad about you, too, Jack. Jack, Jack, will you do something wonderful for me that would make me very happy?

JACK: Well, of course, Marilyn...I'd do anything, anything for you. What is it?

MARILYN: In my next picture, there's going to be so many love scenes, I want you for my leading man.

JACK: Oh, Marilyn, I'd...I'd love to be your leading man.

MARILYN: Good. Now if we can only get permission from Darryl Zanuck.

JACK: Why? Who did Mr. Zanuck have in mind?

MARILYN: Himself.

JACK: Gee, Marilyn, I—I can't get over...the both of us here, all alone on the *Lurilene*.

MARILYN: Yes, Jack, I never dreamed it could happen to I.

JACK: Neither did me.

(Marilyn sighs, as only Marilyn can.)

JACK: Marilyn, why are you sighing?

MARILYN: I was just thinking, Jack, how generous you are. Just so we could be alone on this trip, you chartered the *Lurilene* for $600,000.

JACK: I did?

NARRATOR: If that doesn't wake him up, nothing will.

JACK: Marilyn, Marilyn. I know this is sudden...but...will you...will you marry me?

MARILYN: Marry you? But look at the difference in our ages.

JACK: Well, there isn't much difference, Marilyn—you're 25 and I'm 39.

MARILYN: Yes, but what about 25 years from now, when I'm 50...and you're 39.

JACK: Gee, I never thought of that.

NARRATOR: I did.

JACK: You shut up! Marilyn...Marilyn...will you have dinner with me tonight?

MARILYN: I'd love to, Jack. Thanks, ever so.

JACK: At 8 o'clock.

MARILYN: All right—but I'd better be going now.

(Marilyn sings "Bye, Bye Baby" while Jack holds her in his arms. They kiss passionately. A troubled look clouds Marilyn's face.)

MARILYN: My, that's strange.
JACK: What's strange?
MARILYN: I'm so crazy about you, but that kiss didn't affect me at all!
JACK: That's funny, I'm a wreck!

Jack then awakens to find he's not with Marilyn at all, but with the heavyset woman. He says, "You're not Marilyn Monroe!" She responds, "Well, you ain't no Errol Flynn."

You can't top that!!!

## THE REAL GIRL IN JACK'S LIFE

Over the years on radio and television, Mary Livingstone was many things to Jack—buddy, confidante, critic, conscience, occasional date, poet laureate, straight man, leading lady. The only part that she never played was Jack's wife.

Wait. That's not technically true. She did play the part twice. Once, in a script used on both Jack's radio and television programs, in a dream sequence Jack imagines that he's married to Mary, to disastrous results. After 22 years, Mary is still working at the May Company, while Jack hangs around the house, unemployed, playing his violin and soliciting tips from dinner guests.

The other time was in real life. The story of how they met is familiar to most of us. In 1921, Zeppo Marx invited Jack to a wild party, which turned out to be a Seder at the home of Henry Marks, a distant relative of the Marx Brothers. Henry had a 14-year-old daughter, Sadye, who Jack largely ignored. Jack and Sadye crossed paths several times over the next few years until they met in 1926, and this time Jack noticed her. At first she refused his dating invitations so he started a campaign at Sadye's counter at the May Company, where, by his own telling of the story, he purchased enough hosiery to restock the store and helped Sadye break department sales records.

They were married on January 14, 1927. Their marriage lasted 47 years, until Jack's death in 1974. Mary died in 1983. As Joan Benny tells it, in *Sunday Nights at Seven*, Jack "adored, worshiped and idolized" Mary, in spite of her self-indulgences and "incredible spending habits." "Still," Joan states, in summing up her thoughts on her parents' marriage, "I can't quarrel with success. Whatever the relationship was, it worked for them."

## IN CONCLUSION

Whether her name was Monroe, Mansfield, Lombard, Rutherford, Lamour, Stanwyck, Zybysko, Gearshift, Flapsaddle, or Livingstone, whether you caused us to envy you or to breathe a sigh of relief that it was you and not us, we salute you, Jack Benny, for over 40 years of service to mankind (and womankind). Your genius will survive as long as there remains an audio or video recording of your work, or a memory of hearing a radio broadcast or seeing a TV program. Thank you, Jack, for giving us all a glimpse of that genius.

Maybe we do all have a shot, after all.

Magazine cover 1956. (Kathryn Fuller-Seeley collection)

# Benny's War

## by B. J. Borsody

I t could be argued that the golden age of radio peddled a uniquely American form of propaganda, with Jack Benny being one of its biggest purveyors.

Prior to December of 1941, a new type of consumerism was burgeoning as the United States slogged its way out of the mire of The Great Depression. Factories slowly gasped back to life as new and fantastic synthetic materials such as Lucite and Nylon were displayed at the 1939 World's Fair, itself a symbol of a future ripe with promise and the potential for prosperity. The "Great Melting Pot" took a turn toward Franklin D. Roosevelt's prophesizing that "happy days are here again," even as Hitler prepared to conquer Europe and sterilize all that was not worthy of existence under the oppression of the racially-obsessed Third Reich. Most Americans still had blinders on and were largely oblivious to the suffering and strife in Europe.

By 1943, everyday life was permeated with "The Good War." Healthy young men between 18 and 35 more than likely worked for Uncle Sam, while women took jobs in factories or chaired scrap drives and Red Cross events, joined the WACs, or worked in other ways to support the country and "the boys." The war determined if and how far you traveled, what and how much you ate, and whether a star hung in your window or black crepe on your door. You were admonished to not talk too much, drive too much, or trade in the "Black Market." You faced the war daily on magazine covers, movie newsreels, newspaper headlines, and billboards.

Radio was the single most galvanizing element of the American population during World War II. Churchill's speeches, FDR's "Fireside Chats," and Edward R. Murrow on location in Europe, all crackling over the wireless, brought a major conflict into the living rooms of America's middle class for the first time. This was their war. Their working hours produced planes in the factories and destroyers in the shipyards. Their dollars purchased war bonds. Their sons fought on the front lines.

Radio programming was aimed at this middle-class audience—not at the rich, for whom the war meant increased prosperity, and not at the poor, who worked hard to just survive. The middle-class housewife was the most powerful weapon the American government had in its arsenal, and no one, least of all the sponsors of popular radio programs, was naïve enough to think the war could be won without them.

The groundwork for radio becoming a force in the war effort had been laid well before Hitler's rise to power. Radio stars like Jack Benny, George Burns and Gracie Allen, and Fibber McGee and Molly had endeared themselves to the female American public for years. It was no accident that the majority of these programs were sponsored by food or tobacco manufacturers. Prime time was family time in those days, and Mom (who controlled the household budget) listened in with everyone else. A level of trust had been established between the stars of '40s radio and their audience; people often were unable to distinguish between Jack Benny's radio role and his real-life persona. Many people believed that Jack and Mary really ate Jell-O with dinner or Grape-Nuts for breakfast ("Every time you buy a box of Grape-Nuts Flakes you are saving on ration stamps, because you don't need them!"). Tie that built-in loyalty with patriotism (eating right was a big part of the Home Front Plan), an easily defined enemy, and a product that required no or at least reduced ration points to purchase, and a formula was born that would be the envy of Nike, The Gap, or Budweiser today.

Aside from two definitive instances, little affected the light-hearted fun of *The Jack Benny Program* during the war years. Carole Lombard's death in a plane crash on January 16, 1942 caused Jack to cancel his regular show on January 18 and offer instead a musical presentation with a skeleton cast of Don Wilson and Dennis Day. Benny's show was also canceled on the night of April 15, 1945, when the country mourned the passing of FDR. Yes, the war was there, hovering over the proceedings like an omnipresent ghost, but Jack never lost sight of the fact that his job was to take America's mind off the war as much as possible, if for only a half hour once a week. Even the bombing of Pearl Harbor on December 7, 1941 did not stop the Sunday evening line-up for NBC, save for intermittent news flashes.

The sustaining charm of Benny's program was his willingness to rip a hole in the curtain between performer and audience, and for a moment show the world a glimpse into the making of a radio program, missed cues, flubbed lines, and all. In 1943, the Benny program's lead player was off the air for five weeks due to illness. The force of the personality behind the program was so great that his absence, though notable, was entirely believable. The remaining players needed only to allude to Jack in some manner to keep the momentum going.

For instance, in a discussion between replacement host Orson Welles and Mary Livingstone, Orson discovered that Jack was suffering from such a high fever that he had checked himself into the Biltmore Hotel in Phoenix—a high-tone joint for a man with Jack's reputation for stinginess. Attempts by Orson to reach Jack at the Biltmore came up empty, as "his temperature went down and he checked out." Jack had relocated to the Jasmine Blossom Auto Court, whose monogrammed towels matched his initials, and whose rates, one imagined, were more in keeping with his austere lifestyle. Jack didn't say a word, yet his presence was felt in every line of the script. When he returned to the program there was no stumbling around for him to reestablish his place in the cast, when for all practical purposes he had never been away. For five weeks the show ran seamlessly without its title character, the audience manipulated into believing an illusion.

In a similar way, the show propagandized for the sake of the war effort. Radio scripts were embedded with war propaganda; in time, listeners came to believe that everyone across the country followed the rationing rules, pitched in on scrap drives, bought war bonds. On Benny's show, humor masked the message.

With Jack gone, Rochester called Orson Welles to complain that the pork chops "I had to use commando tactics to obtain" were about to be turned into chop suey by Orson's cook, Chong.

> ORSON: You are treating those pork chops like they were radium.
> ROCHESTER: I can get radium tomorrow. Let's see you try and go get a pork chop.

The theme continued after Benny's return:

> JACK: Remember we have rationing now, so I can't dish out food like I used to.
> MARY: Like you used to?
> JACK: Yes.
> MARY: You got so many meals out of a leg of lamb one time, it got mad and kicked you.

Most Americans could relate to these exchanges. The middle class had made unprecedented sacrifices for the soldiers and would continue doing so for two more years. One can't underestimate the effects that radio comedy had on the public morale. Who could gripe about rationing if big stars like Orson Welles and Jack Benny felt the pinch too? Even if the sacrifices were being made behind the "fourth wall" of radio make-believe.

As with other shows broadcast during the war years, Benny's occasionally waved the patriotic flag, sometimes for the duration of an entire episode. The show, however, never crossed the delicate line between patriotism and crass cultural lampooning.

After Pearl Harbor the American public embraced the war. An environment of ethnocentric pride developed, engendering unfortunate prejudicial tendencies in some quarters. Depictions of the Germans, Italians, and Japanese as evil or incompetent were rampant. The suffering of Japanese-Americans in internment camps has since been documented and condemned. *The Jack Benny Program* had its share of ethnic characters wandering in and out of the weekly scripts, but they were treated with respect, warmth, and affection.

Jack's unabashed spirit of patriotism and faith in America were evidenced in his New Year's Eve episodes. Jack and Mary took part in the annual play, acting the roles of The Old Year and Columbia (The Spirit of America). The 1943 show (airing on January 2, 1944) opens to the strains of "Auld Lang Syne." Phil Harris appears as Uncle Sam, Don Wilson as the U.S. Navy (doubling his tonnage that year), and jokes abound regarding current events and personalities such as Eleanor Roosevelt and Frank Sinatra.

The skit slowly turns serious as The Old Year switches on the radio to listen to the World Series. The events of World War II are played out in that most revered of American pastimes—baseball. The United Nations All-Stars are up against the Axis Polecats. The war becomes a simple game of right versus wrong, good versus evil. Heavy hitters—Montgomery, MacArthur, and Chiang Kai-shek—bat for God's team, while the bumbling Axis players argue amongst themselves. Just as Eisenhower comes to bat, Columbia and Uncle Sam make The Old Year turn off the broadcast. It is time for him to depart.

"I want to hear the end of the game."

"I know how you feel Old Timer, but you just haven't got the time."

"Okay, okay. Turn off the radio. I've got a good idea how it is going to turn out anyhow."

Strong words. The tide of Allied victory didn't truly turn until 1944, and the path to Axis defeat wasn't apparent until 1945. As Baby New Year appears carrying "Unconditional Surrender" documents he hopes to get signed in 1944, he receives instructions from The Old Year that there is a big game going on, and when it is over it will be 1944's responsibility to "clean up the field and put it in order again."

"Taps" begins to play softly in the background, and The Old Year explains that it's for the players who were put out early in the game when the pitching was a little too fast for them. It wasn't their fault. Tojo started pitching before the umpire cried "Play Ball!" And that "ain't baseball, son. Not like they play it in America." Old Year '43 tells Baby '44 to remember the name Collin Kelly, who represented all the boys who got only one turn at bat. Finally, 1943 departs with a shaky "Keep 'em Flyin'," referring to both war planes and American flags.

Yes, it was propaganda. It was underscored, however, with a conviction and sincerity impossible to duplicate today. Jack Benny represented an image of America that began dying out after the war, and he maintained that image through the turbulent decades that followed despite rapidly changing times and morals.

Perhaps our entertainers find their place in certain times and settings for a reason. Perhaps World War II could have been won without the talents of Jack Benny, Bob Hope, George Burns, and Fred Allen. Perhaps not. Sadly, these great talents wouldn't be able to make it in today's over-the-top comic environment where four-letter words and "in your face" humor rule the day. But few, if any, of today's comedians could have matched up with Jack Benny during the Golden Age of Radio.

There is a time and place for everything...and everyone.

# Cheapskate Benny or Generous Jack?

## by Charles A. Beckett

First-time listeners to Jack Benny's radio show quickly learn that the character Benny portrayed was that of a self-centered cheapskate. He bought gasoline for his Maxwell a gallon at a time. While on vacation he made extra money by working as a towel boy on the beach or as a bellhop in the hotel. After a bad game of golf, he demanded a refund for the lessons he'd taken from the professional, and if he lost a ball he'd make Rochester scour the woods until it was found.

The Benny character gave tips reluctantly, using foreign coins, coupons, stamps, tokens, or anything other than United States currency. On rare occasions when he did tip with a real nickel or dime, he received indignant responses from the recipients. The one instance in which he tipped generously—fifty cents to panhandler John L. C. Sivoney—turned into a gag that ran for weeks.

Members of his cast grew accustomed to receiving Christmas gifts of a single golf ball, shoe laces, a used gopher trap. When he bought a 90-cent G-string for his violin, he insisted on charging it.

Next door neighbor Ronald Colman was Benny's source of water, electricity, eggs, butter, and sugar. Benny borrowed Colman's newspaper from his front stoop and had Rochester sneak it back after he'd read it.

When Jack had lunch with his "gang" at the drugstore, he usually found a way to avoid picking up the check. When he did "fight" for the check, he knew precisely when to withdraw and say, "Well, if you insist."

While out of town, he allowed the milkman to graze his horse on the front lawn—for a fee. Other times, Dennis Day mowed Jack's grass. He had to. It was in his contract. On one occasion, when Benny was being particularly tightfisted, Rochester chided him with, "You can't take it with you," to which Benny responded, "If I can't take it with me, I won't go."

A prime example of Jack Benny's on-air love of money arose when he was accosted by a hold-up man. "Your money or your life." Silent pause. The would-be mugger repeated, "Your money or your life, bud!" Then came Jack's studied reply: "I'M THINKING IT OVER!"

The Benny character's stinginess was legend. In one episode, he sneaked into a Radio City 60-cent tour, without paying. Upon entering Fred Allen's studio, the tour guide confronted Benny. Allen came to Benny's rescue, offering to pay the 60 cents. Jack said, "Wait a minute, Fred. Put that money away. I've only seen half the tour. Give him 30 cents." When Benny thanked Allen for paying the 30 cents, Allen replied, "Oh, it was nothing," to which Jack shot back with, "Nothing, he says. Thirty cents!"

When in Las Vegas, the real Jack Benny enjoyed playing the slot machines, usually the half-dollar ones. Harrah's Casino, as a gag, bought a machine that took only pennies. They brought it out only when Benny appeared there, hanging a sign on it that read "For Jack Benny's use only." Another tribute to his famous and unshakable reputation as a cheapskate.

Cheapness was an important part of Benny's radio personality, but was he cheap in real life? Of course not. Nonetheless, throughout his life Jack fought—without success—to live down his public reputation as a cheapskate.

Benny's producer, Hillard Marks, recalled a taxi-driver refusing a generous tip from Jack with the plea, "Please, Mister Benny, don't disillusion me." Jack once remarked that "no other phase of my image has the longevity and the laugh-arousing power of the stinginess."

In reality, Benny was the opposite of his radio character. People who knew him described him as being one of the most modest and generous people in show business. Cast members often spoke of how generous and good Jack Benny had been to them. Phil Harris remembered that "Me and the other cast members were making so much money we didn't know what to do with it. We didn't have to work for anyone else. About every six months, Jack would tell Blume, his manager, to give me more money. I said I didn't need any more money, that I appreciated Jack's getting me off the road. I would have three lines on a show, and Jack would say 'Go tell Blume to give you some more money.'"

Eddie "Rochester" Anderson also benefited from Benny's generosity. Within two years of his first appearance on Benny's show, Anderson made enough money to live in a mansion with his wife Maymie and his family—and employ three servants. He was financially able to enjoy the hobbies of raising thoroughbred horses and road racing in custom-built sports cars.

Ray Kemper, a sound man on Benny's television programs, recalled getting a check from Benny "every week, over and above my CBS salary. Not many stars did that in those days. Jack Benny was a kind and generous man."

In 1942, Jack made the movie *George Washington Slept Here*. A Warner Bros. representative gave Hillard Marks an envelope with $6,000 in it—expense money for the cast's return trip from the movie's New York premiere. Marks remembered it as the most lavish train ride Benny and company ever took. "But we still couldn't spend all the money. At Jack's insistence, we shared the cash with porters and conductors across the country."

Benny was also generous with his time and talent, raising money for worthy causes. In January of 1950 he took his cast to New York to kick off a campaign for the American Heart Association, to raise six million dollars for heart research, education, and community services. At the end of the performance, still in character, he said, "Don't worry, folks. I don't get any of the money. They just promised to let me count it." At another radio benefit, Jack announced on the air that, as their price of admission, everyone in the audience had donated a pint of blood to the Red Cross.

During the 1950s and '60s, symphony orchestras experienced severe financial problems. In 1956, Carnegie Hall was one of those in difficulty. Jack gave a benefit violin performance—accompanied by the New York Philharmonic Symphony Orchestra—for the Committee to Save Carnegie Hall, as well as the

National Association for Retarded Children. During the next 18 years, his concerts raised almost six million dollars for musicians' pension funds and saved several symphonies from bankruptcy.

In 1958, he played a concert in Kansas City to aid the city's struggling symphony orchestra. Weeks before his arrival in Missouri, the 2,500-seat Municipal Auditorium was sold out. He had raised $55,000 before playing one note—wiping out the orchestra's entire deficit. President Truman, master of ceremonies that evening and an able pianist, said he would not be playing any duets with Jack Benny. "After all," he quipped, "we don't want to run the risk of having to return all the money."

During World War II, Benny's generosity showed itself in his support of American military service personnel. In May of 1941, he aired his first radio show from a military base. From that time through December, 1946, he broadcast from more than 35 Army, Navy, Marine, and Air Corps camps, stations, and airfields, as well as from an aircraft carrier and several military hospitals. And, at the end of the 1942 radio season, he spent thirteen weeks of his summer vacation touring and performing at military bases across the country, accompanied by various guest stars, at his own expense. In July, 1943, he began a nine-week USO tour to entertain American and British troops in Africa, Egypt, the Persian Gulf, Italy, and elsewhere. Benny performed wherever he found a group of military personnel, large or small, congregated.

In the spring of '44, he went to Canada to participate in their sixth Victory Loan Drive to help raise the millions of dollars needed to fund Canada's war efforts. For five days, Jack and his cast made appearances at bond rallies, shipyards, military bases, and hospitals. On the first day alone, Benny raised nearly three million dollars for the war effort. Nine thousand people filled the halls and galleries of the Hastings Park Forum for the broadcast of the Jack Benny radio show from Vancouver, British Columbia. Benny personally paid all expenses for his group's transportation, hotel bills, and wire charges for the broadcast.

After his last broadcast of the 1944 season, Benny once again headed up a 21-day USO troupe to Australian bases and military hospitals, followed by five weeks of shows in New Guinea and Hawaii. He even provided shows to small groups of military personnel on remote islands.

During the Korean Conflict of the early 1950s, Benny's radio programs were broadcast periodically from military installations and hospitals. In 1951, he led a USO tour with harmonica player Larry Adler and others to entertain American military troops stationed in Korea.

According to Mary Livingstone, Jack was "the most generous man. He was constantly giving me sentimental gifts. All my jewelry is engraved with beautiful, thoughtful words. He even gave me presents on *his* birthday." Benny's daughter Joan said of him, "He was certainly never cheap with my mother or me; nor with anyone else, for that matter. Nor did he forget birthdays, anniversaries, Valentine's Day, Easter, or any other excuse to buy a gift. I can't imagine a man more generous and thoughtful than my father." George Burns summed up

Benny's financial persona when he said, "The whole miser thing was a made-up gimmick to get laughs. Jack never cared about money. He would think nothing of writing a check for $25,000 for charity. I don't think he ever did really know how much he had. He never worried about it."

Audiences loved to laugh at Jack Benny's parsimonious character on radio, TV, and in the movies. People who knew him were well aware of what a truly thoughtful, giving, and generous man he was in real life.

Only in his dreams did Jack envision this dollar bill,
found in a Hollywood memorabilia store in 1994.

When the price of stamps hit 39 cents in 2006, Laura Leff, president of the International Jack Benny
Fan Club, led the "Thirty-nine Man March" on Washington, D.C. in an effort to persuade members of
Congress to issue a stamp honoring Jack. The stamp seen here was part of a set issued in 1994. Others
honored with Benny at the time with likenesses on stamps were Fanny Brice, Edgar Bergen and
Charlie McCarthy, Abbott and Costello, and Laurel and Hardy.

# Balzer on Benny

## by Jordan R. Young

*Editor's Note: George Balzer died Sept. 28, 2006, at age 91, as this book was about to go to press.*

For a writer who spent over three decades in Hollywood, George Balzer did not have a great number of credits to his name. The reason: Jack Benny. While Balzer scripted programs for Bob Burns, Lucille Ball, Red Skelton, George Burns and Gracie Allen, and Don Knotts, he spent most of his career writing for Benny. There are worse things a comedy writer could have on his resume.

The two-time Emmy winner ("two and a half" by his count) was reluctant to be interviewed when I first called him in 1989; he told me he had a book in the works about his experiences with Benny and didn't particularly want to talk. He then followed with several impromptu comments. When the last of his statements was followed by a silence, he caught on. "Did you get that all down?" he asked. "Yes," I assured him, as I finished scribbling.

Balzer finally agreed to an interview in 1992, having abandoned his book project. Regrettably, he was unable to find a publisher; Milt Josefsberg, Irving Fein, and others had beaten him to the punch line. The following is extracted from my book, *The Laugh Crafters: Comedy Writing in Radio and TV's Golden Age.*

*Did you intend to write for radio, or did you get into it purely by chance?*

I never did any writing, actually, until I started to write comedy. That came about because I had an opportunity to listen to a lot of radio, comedy radio. I just kind of felt that maybe I could write that kind of material. So I gave it a try. And strangely enough, coming out of that period (1937) of listening a lot, I started to write my first script. I wrote my version of *The Jack Benny Show.* The coincidence of what happened is kind of interesting. I started out of the blue to write *Jack Benny* scripts, just for my own amusement…

*I believe you were a protégé of Sam Perrin's?*

That's correct, yes. Sam and I were partners for—oh, my gosh—probably 35 years. When I went to work on *Burns and Allen,* Sam was brought on staff at the same time. So we met, everything worked out well, and we wound up with Jack Benny.

*Would George Burns usually come up with a premise for his show, or would one of the writers?*

I'm sure he did. I don't recall a particular—I'm sure that George had ideas, the same as Jack had ideas. But Jack Benny never regarded himself as a writer.

He would get ideas. One time I remember he came in, and he said, "Fellas, last night I was watching television. And I watched the Marquis Chimps. I think it would be funny if we could somehow use them on one of our programs." And I looked at him and I said, "Yeah—then what?" He said, "Well, I don't know, that's up to you, fellas." And he turned and walked out of the room. And as he reached the door Jack turned and said, "I wouldn't have your job for a million dollars."

*Pretty funny, especially considering Benny's "anything for a buck" persona.*

Strangely enough, it was a good basic thought. And about an hour later—we kicked it around a little bit—an hour later, I went into Jack's office and I said, "Jack, how about this?" And I loosely outlined an idea that would hold the show together, with the Chimps.

*Benny did more with absolutely nothing than anybody.*

Yeah. Jack knew comedy so well that he was able to play on and extend the comedy that was there. As Jack himself used to say, "I know that when I say, 'Well…' that that's not funny unless I've got something leading up to it that's really strong." He's right. The word "Well…" without some situation or line doesn't mean a thing. And Jack appreciated that. He regarded his writers—he said to me, "I'm number one because it's my show, and I'm the star. Then after me come my four writers. After my writers come the parking lot attendant, the shoeshine boy, the janitor, my director, the producer—and you can put them in any order you want to put them. But don't put anybody between me and my writers." And for that simple philosophy, Jack Benny became known in the business as a genius.

*That attitude must have endeared him to his staff.*

All he did was—he hired and paid good money for what he felt was good talent *for him,* and he let us perform. All told, I was with Jack 25 years. Sam Perrin, the same thing. Milt Josefsberg was with the show 12 years, so he had a nice run too. John Tackaberry was there 12 years. Jack never forgot he had writers. But his success was due to his own talent.

*How did "Anaheim, Azusa, and Cucamonga" develop?*

Well, it just came about—we were going to go to New York, and we were going to do a scene at the railroad station. Union Station. Leaving for New York, catching the Super Chief. And we just used that as an interesting and funny thing to have happen while we were at the railway station. So just as Jack and Mary opened the doors, and you heard the crowd noises, you heard, "Train leaving on Track 5 for Anaheim, Azusa, and Cuc…amonga." We did a joke or two as the show went on, and that was the end of that. We were only going to use it one show.

*These were names that you picked off the map?*

No. I'm almost a native here—I came out from Pennsylvania when I was four years old—I know all these towns. So when it came that we wanted to do this, I said, "Use Anaheim, Azusa, and…"—I think the first one was, "Anaheim, Azusa, and Pomona." But at rehearsal Jack said, "I don't know, I don't think that's quite right." I said, "How about Cucamonga?" He said, "Yeah, that'll work, we'll do that."

*I believe you were also the one who dreamed up the "I Can't Stand Jack Benny Because…" contest.*

We needed a show, Tuesday came along and we just couldn't get started. We didn't have anything on paper. Sunday was approaching and we didn't know what to do. We finally got a little bit of an idea where someone said, "Why don't we ask the listeners to send in lyrics, and then we'll have Mahlon Merrick, the conductor, set them to music and have a little contest…" And Jack said, "No, no, I don't want to do that." So I said, "You know, Jack, I have an idea. Nowadays all we hear on the radio is, 'I like so-and-so toothpaste because…' in 25 words or less. Why don't we do 'I can't stand Jack Benny' in 25 words or less? We'll ask people to write in letters from all over the country." Well, there was silence in the room. Dead silence. And I begin to think to myself, "Uh-oh."

*Better go look for a job.*

Jack got up out of his chair and he came over to me and put his hand on my shoulder and he said, "That's it. That's what we're going to do." I said, "Jack…" He says, "No, no, we're going to do it. Only we're gonna give $10,000 as the prize." And we did. We were looking for one show; it ran for eleven consecutive weeks. We had a winner, of course, who got the money—the winning letter was read by Ronald Colman. Fred Allen, Goodman Ace, and Peter Lorre were the judges in the contest. And we had to hire eight girls to sort the mail. So it was very successful.

*Jack Benny was probably the only star in Hollywood who would…*

…have enough guts to do it.

*Anyone else would have too much ego to even consider it.*

That's right. I had an occasion when I first joined the show—I think I was there about three months—we were at NBC in Hollywood, and we were doing the rewrite on a Saturday rehearsal. Just kind of cleaning it up and cutting it down to time for Sunday's show. And Jack came to a page, and he says, "Fellas, I want a new joke here." We all turned to that page. He said, "I want something stronger. Something that'll really button this whole thing up." We don't say a word. He kept talking. He said, "I want something that *really* pays this off." After a pause—I was sitting next to him—I touched his arm and I said, "Jack, we'll get you a new joke." He says, "Ohhh, you agree with me, huh?" I said, "No, but it's possible that the four of us could be wrong." He looked at me, he broke into a laugh—literally slid right off his chair and sat in the corner screaming. And he got up, and he said, "I wouldn't change that joke now for a million dollars." And he didn't. And it got its big laugh. We're all standing in the booth, and he looked up at us—as if to say, "You smart-alecks." That's the kind of a man he was.

*The gag about the robber confronting him—"Your money or your life?"—has become the quintessential Jack Benny joke.*

What happened was that John Tackaberry and Milt Josefsberg had been working on a script for Jack, their part of a script for Jack, and they had come to a point where they had the line, "Your money or your life?" And that stopped them. They couldn't get an answer for the question. Tack is stretched out on the couch, and Milt is pacing up and down, trying to get a follow for "Your money or your life?" And he gets a little peeved at Tack, and he says, "For God sakes, Tack, say something." Tack—maybe he was half asleep—in defense of himself, says, "I'm thinking it over." And Milt says, "Wait a minute. That's it." And that's the line that went in the script.

*It's one of the classic moments in radio history.*

By the way, that was *not* the biggest laugh that Jack ever got. It has the reputation of getting the biggest laugh. But that's not true...

*What would you say the biggest laugh was?*

The biggest laugh? I *know* what the biggest laugh was. It was just by coincidence. It was a very short line that I threw, because the situation was building so—that was when we had [opera singer] Dorothy Kirsten on the radio show. When she came on our stage, she met the members of our cast, and she met Don Wilson. Just the night before she had given a concert here in Los Angeles. And Don, being the educated one of our cast, started talking to her about music, and he said, "Miss Kirsten, I thought it was absolutely astounding when you did so-and-so"—he used all the musical terms, the *obbligato*, the *crescendo*—and she says, "Well, I don't quite agree with you in every respect. I thought the..."—and she had her string of beautiful musical terms. This went back and forth. And Jack, who's been standing there all this time, said, "Well, I thought..." And Mary said, "Oh, shut up." That's all she said. Mary delivered that line perfectly. The laugh ran 29 seconds. As long as Jack looked at that [studio] audience, they laughed. "Your money or your life?" got seven seconds—the original delivery.

*Milt Josefsberg said you had a flair for wild humor. Could you elaborate on that? Or maybe you don't agree with it.*

No, I do agree with it. I used to come up with things that were a little on the wild side. This isn't wild, but it might give you an idea—it's a little wild. One time Phil Harris came in and he was late for the rehearsal, and he excused himself. He says, "I'm sorry, Jackson [Jack], I couldn't get my car started, so I had to come over here on the bus." Jack says, "On the bus? Phil, you come over here on the bus, like *that?*" Phil says, "Well, how do you like that? I put on a glove that was holding a Scotch and soda."

*I believe Milt Josefsberg quoted you as saying, "If a writer didn't cause Jack to send his suit to the cleaners, he wasn't earning his money."*

When we first went to New York and joined Jack for the very first time, we went to the Sherry-Netherland Hotel to start writing the script, and Jack at that time was trying to get off cigars. And so he had a pipe, which he didn't put tobacco in; he just kept it in his mouth. As we worked, and the minutes and the hours went on, naturally saliva accumulated in the bowl of that pipe. And if you came up with a really good joke, he would come over and put his left hand on your right shoulder, and with his other hand he would just kind of wave that pipe up and down and laugh. You'd begin to notice after a while that there was a stream that would run from your left shoulder down to your waist on the right. One day I said, "You know, if you leave this room looking like an ambassador, you've had a good day."

*Could you discuss your strengths and weaknesses as a comedy writer, compared to the others on Benny's staff—Sam Perrin, Milt Josefsberg, John Tackaberry? Would you each specialize in a particular type of joke?*

Well, not really. Maybe to this extent—Milt and Tack were a little jokier than Sam and myself. They could bump into somebody on the street and stand there and tell five jokes. Whereas Sam and I usually wrote picture. Word picture. And got our comedy out of the situation and the questions and answers. I could do most anything. But then I guess when you come right down to it, if we had to, maybe any one of us could do the show for a week without too much difficulty.

*The Benny show—the writers at least—really had a penchant for visual jokes.*

Yeah, I guess we did—we used anything that would build the best picture. We really were bent that way. I know that when it came to doing pictures alone, with television, Sam Perrin and I moved right in, kind of headed up the television show. We just switched on over—for a while we did both the radio and television shows.

*Did Benny seem to adapt to television pretty easily?*

Yeah. Took about 20 minutes, I think. Sam and I made the transition to TV with Jack; we did the first several shows. Milt Josefsberg and the other guys stayed in radio—they were more prone to start something and get into a stand-up routine. But Sam and I did most of the TV work. You can't always tell this by credits, because in those days, there were no credits. The Writer's Guild was not organized. A couple of the writers were unhappy with having to stay in radio, so we juggled the credits around, where everything would look better.

*Could you assess Benny as a radio comedian, as opposed to his work in other media? Why did radio capture him best?*

First, he had a perfect voice. The voice was just great. And he could handle radio the best. Although I feel that on most of his television shows he was good—maybe on many he was very good—he was always better on radio.

*The Benny shows still hold up remarkably well, undiminished by age.*

We played to a studio audience. And any reaction we got was legit. Once in a while you fixed up a joke because the audience couldn't see the bit, or couldn't hear it or something—but when Jack came out to do a monologue or a bit or whatever, that was it. You either laughed or you didn't. And fortunately, they laughed most of the time.

*Reprinted from* The Laugh Crafters: Comedy Writing in Radio and TV's Golden Age *by Jordan R. Young, Past Times Publishing, 1999.*

# To Be or Not to Be: Jack Benny in Hollywood 1940-1945

## by Philip G. Harwood

JACK BENNY: You made *Sonny Boy,* which was one of Warner Brothers' first talkies.

AL JOLSON: And you made *The Horn Blows at Midnight,* which was nearly their last!

(from *The Jack Benny Program,* May 18, 1947)

Jack Benny was a major success on radio and television and was considered one of the great comedians of the 20th century. But, although he appeared in close to thirty movies, he felt satisfied with just three of his films and loved only one.

He advised people to avoid the movies he'd made prior to 1940. Today, those films are hard to find anyway, so not to worry. Some years ago, MGM/UA released *George Washington Slept Here* and *The Horn Blows at* Midnight. Both are now out of print, to be found in libraries or through catalogs offering the old and obscure, or maybe on television from time to time. His beloved *To Be or Not to Be* and later movies in which he had walk-on roles (*Gypsy, It's A Mad, Mad, Mad, Mad World,* A *Guide For the Married Man*) are available on DVD.

You'd have to know a serious collector in order to view early Benny movies like *Transatlantic Merry-Go-Round, The Hollywood Revue of 1929,* or *Broadway Melody of 1936.* Even the classic *Charley's Aunt* is hard to find these days.

Benny yearned for challenging movie roles; he didn't want to merely play himself, rehashing in movies what he did each week on his radio program. By 1940, Jack's success in radio led to a demand for him to start a movie career. He dabbled in Jack Benny-character outings, capitalizing on his feud with Fred Allen in *Love Thy Neighbor* and *It's in the Bag.* Those films were made to appeal to his radio fans.

His other movies of this era, however, saw Jack playing characters unlike the one familiar to radio listeners. He was allowed to spread his wings and follow his celluloid dreams.

*Charley's Aunt* was first portrayed by W. S. Penley in 1892 on the British stage. In 1915, a silent film version of the play was produced, reprised ten years later with Charles Chaplin's brother, Sydney, in the title role. Charles Ruggles appeared in the 1930 early sound version and Arthur Ashley appeared in the 1940 British spoof, *Charley's Big-Hearted Aunt.* In 1949, Ray Bolger appeared in a musical stage version, *Where's Charley?,* which was made into a movie in 1952.

The *Charley's Aunt* in which Benny appeared was shot in 1941. Archie Mayo directed the George Perlberg production. Jack portrayed Babbs Babberley, a student who for ten years has been trying to pass a three-year course at Oxford. After accidentally knocking down the proctor, he is in danger of being expelled. He avoids expulsion by making a deal with two campus roommates, Charley

(Richard Haydn) and Jack (James Ellison). They agree to lie on Babbs's behalf if he'll pose as Charley's Aunt.

*Charley's Aunt* (1941); Jack Benny with Kay Francis (courtesy of Laura Leff)

*Charley's Aunt* (1941); Belgian poster. (from the Philip Harwood collection)

Although his British accent drifted off here and there, Jack did well with the role. He favored his part in *Charley's Aunt*, but the critics weren't so impressed. According to Jack, "one critic claimed that so much of my own personality came through that I should have been billed as Jacqueline Benny."

Jack's fortunes turned when German director Ernst Lubitsch, known for his sophisticated film comedies *Design for Living* and *Ninotchka*, offered him the part of Joseph Tura in *To Be or Not to Be*. The role, according to the director, had been written with Jack in mind. Lubitsch had made Garbo laugh, so getting Jack Benny to act in a serious production appeared to be within his capabilities.

*To Be or Not to Be* is set in Poland, 1939. Joseph Tura and his wife Maria (Carole Lombard) are starring in an anti-Nazi stage play. The Nazis march in and replace the play with a production of Shakespeare's *Hamlet*. Maria becomes smitten with a Polish fighter pilot, Sobinski (Robert Stack), who is called to duty when Germany invades Poland. Sobinski goes to England where he learns of a Nazi plot to destroy the Polish resistance movement. Tura and his troupe become involved in the effort to save the resistance.

*To Be or Not to Be* (1942); Production shot of Joseph Tura on stage. (courtesy of Laura Leff)

Jack once said that Lubitsch "was about the only director who ever really directed me. In practically all my earlier pictures the director would say, 'Jack, you know so much more about comedy than I do, play the scene the way you feel like.' The only trouble was that I knew lots about radio comedy, a little about stage comedy, but nothing about movies." Jack said that Lubitsch wanted him to forget everything he knew about screen acting and start fresh. During filming, Lubitsch would act out a scene to show Jack what he wanted. According to Jack, Lubitsch "was a lousy actor, but a great director."

Although Joseph Tura will always be a ham (as is seen at the end of the film), Jack portrays a heroic figure who stands against the Nazis. Lubitsch, in *To Be or Not to Be,* doesn't shy away from chances to pillory Nazi tyranny as he presents the Polish people as brave patriots.

*To Be or Not to Be* (1942); Jack as Toura as Hamlet (Philip Harwood collection)

The chemistry between Carole Lombard and Jack is strong. Lombard was coming into her own as a screen comedian. With such films as *Nothing Sacred* and *My Man Godfrey* behind her, she had just finished filming *Mr. and Mrs. Smith*, a rare screwball comedy for the master of suspense, Alfred Hitchcock.

It was Jack who recommended Lombard for the role of Maria and arranged for a script to be sent to her. Lombard knew Lubitsch from their days at Paramount in the early 1930s. She jumped at the chance to do *To Be or Not to Be*, not only to work with Lubitsch, but because the movie spoke out against global terrorism. Lombard repaid Jack's favor by helping him with his challenging role.

Filming was in progress when Japan attacked Pearl Harbor on December 7, 1941. By Christmas Eve, *To Be or Not to Be* was completed. Lombard wanted to do her part for the war effort, so immediately after the filming she embarked on a tour to sell war bonds. With her mother accompanying her, she made several stops around the country. She never returned home to her husband, Clark Gable, however, for she and all aboard her plane perished in a fiery crash in the mountains near Lake Tahoe.

Jack was devastated. "She was one of the few gals you could love as a woman, and treasure as a friend," he later said. Lombard was to have been the guest star on Jack's next radio show. He cancelled the broadcast altogether.

What should have been a glorious opening to an entertaining and historically significant movie turned out to be painfully somber. Neither the public nor the critics were able to deny the dreadful circumstances surrounding the making of the picture and the death of Lombard. The movie suffered at the box office.

*To Be or Not to Be* (1942); Dutch poster (Philip Harwood collection)

Jack's father, Meyer Kubelsky, almost single-handedly brought ticket sales to a respectable level, though his initial reaction to the movie was hardly what Jack expected. When the proud father first saw his son wearing a Nazi uniform and shouting "Heil Hitler," he stood up and left the theatre. When he later told Jack of his shame at seeing him wearing a Nazi uniform and giving the Nazi salute, Jack told of the goodness of his character and how he ended up foiling the Nazi party. He pleaded with his father to return to the theater and see the film all the way through. Meyer went to a town where no one knew him and watched the film. Jack said later that his father saw *To Be or Not to Be* 46 times. Now *there's* a dedicated father!

The promotional trailer for Jack's next picture, *George Washington Slept Here,* is unique. It begins not with scenes from the film, but with Jack in a Warner Brothers screening room viewing scenes from Ann Sheridan films, including on-screen smooching with Ronald Reagan in *Juke Girl* and James Cagney in *City For Conquest.* Jack feels that he can kiss just as well as Ann's other male leads. He begs Jack Warner for an on-screen kiss with the "Oomph girl." The answer is no. Not even a little one.

*George Washington Slept Here* (1942) (Philip Harwood collection)

*George Washington Slept Here* was the forerunner of such films as *The Egg and I, Mr. Blandings Builds His Dream House,* and, more recently, *The Money Pit.* Couple buys dilapidated home, have nervous breakdown trying to renovate it.

In the 1940 George Kaufman/Moss Hart play, Ernest Truex and Jean Dixon portrayed the Fullers. Mr. Fuller, a history enthusiast and collector of antiques, convinces his wife to agree to the purchase of an old farmhouse in which George

Washington supposedly slept. They're forced to deal with rotting floors, no running water, leaky roofs, goofy relatives, and annoying neighbors.

Jack noticed that in the Broadway play, the wife had all the funny lines. His head was also turned by character actor Percy Kilbride, portraying caretaker/handyman Mr. Kimber. Before signing on to make the film, Jack had two matters of importance to talk over with Jack Warner.

First, if Jack was to star in the film, he had to have the funny lines. Switching the roles took care of that; the wife (Ann Sheridan) became the antique enthusiast; Jack portrayed the disgruntled and frustrated city-loving husband.

The other matter was Percy Kilbride. Jack had been floored by Kilbride's deadpan comedic approach, and he wanted to bring him to Warner Brothers for a screen test. Jack Warner said the studio had enough character actors; he wasn't interested in Kilbride. Jack insisted, offering to pay the expenses. That did the trick, and Kilbride was hired. Little did Jack know how difficult, though enjoyable, life would soon be with Kilbride on the set.

Jack had a terrific sense of humor and when something struck him as funny, he was known to literally drop in a heap to the floor, shaking with laughter. Kilbride had this effect on him, to the extent that Jack found it hard to work with him. Whenever he tested with Kilbride, Jack burst out laughing. During filming, thirty or more takes were needed for a scene. Finally, director William Keighley said Jack would be dropped from the film if the hysterics continued. Jack's solution: the night before filming he wouldn't go to bed, so the next morning he would be exhausted and not have the strength to laugh at Kilbride. (Kilbride, of course, was to later find fame in *The Egg and I* with Fred MacMurray and Claudette Colbert before moving on to star with Marjorie Main in the *Ma and Pa Kettle* film series.)

The theme music for *George Washington Slept Here* was supposed to have been sung. Adolph Deutsch, composer of film scores for *The Maltese Falcon, High Sierra,* and *Northern Pursuit,* wrote a comical score for *George Washington Slept Here* with the following lyrics:

> *The books all say a Gen'ral came this way,*
> *He took off his shoes to have a snooze,*
> *Ding! Dong!*
> *It's very clear, George Washington slept here.*
> *The proof we found, right on this very ground*
> *He didn't count sheep, far and near,*
> *George Washington slept here.*
> *If he had decided to stay up,*
> *The price of this antique would not be way up.*
> *To bed, to bed, a very sleepy head!*
> *Turned in for the night, blew out the light*
> *On eight hours sleep,*
> *How could he fight?*
> *Ding! Dong!*

*Give him a rousing cheer*
*George Washington slept here.*
(Lyricist unknown; courtesy of Marco Polo Records)

The main title sequence was shortened during post-production editing, so the theme song was abandoned. But with these lyrics you can now try singing along the next time you see the movie.

Toward the end of the film, after many mishaps and disasters, the Fullers learn that they owe back-taxes on the home. If not paid, the bank will foreclose. The Fullers argue, and in the midst of the argument, Mr. Fuller falls down a flight of stairs. The next scene cuts to Mr. Fuller with a compress on his head. Still shots exist of the Fullers dressed as George and Martha Washington, from an eliminated dream sequence that occurred before Mr. Fuller is seen with the compress.

Jack's next stage adaptation was *The Meanest Man in the World*, filmed at Twentieth Century-Fox in 1943. Jack was supposedly trying to veer away from his radio persona, but in the prelude, what do you hear? Why, it's "Love in Bloom." And who appears as Jack's assistant, but Eddie "Rochester" Anderson. Jack portrays Richard Clark, an extremely nice lawyer. When he falls in love with Priscilla Lane, his future father-in-law makes him an offer: become a successful lawyer in New York, and you can marry Priscilla. After initially failing in New York, Clark realizes that to be a success, he must become a heel: stealing candy from a child, evicting a woman, getting slapped by his girlfriend. Each incident is photographed for the daily newspapers.

*The Meanest Man in the World* is one of Jack's shortest feature films, clocking in at fifty-seven minutes. A running gag—whenever an ambulance siren is heard, all lawyers run out of their offices at once—is quite amusing, but the movie's drawbacks are hard to ignore. Anne Revere, known for her matronly roles in such films as *National Velvet* and *Gentleman's Agreement*, seems wasted in the role as the secretary who secretly pines for Richard. And Priscilla Lane seems too young for Jack's character.

*The Meanest Man in the World* (1943);
Jack Benny with Priscilla Lane (Philip Harwood collection)

Jack did two more films for Warner Brothers in 1945. One was a cameo in an all-star extravaganza entitled *Hollywood Canteen*. Jack was thrilled to be in this film; not only was he doing his part for the war effort, but he had a scene with one of the world's great violinists, Joseph Szigeti.

And then came *The Horn Blows at Midnight*. Oh, what havoc this little comedy would bring to Jack's world. He plays Athanael, a radio studio musician who falls asleep and dreams he is an angel sent to earth to signal the end of the world with a blast of his trumpet.

It's a goofy comedy and has its moments, but it arrived at theaters to find a public bored with fantasy. Other fantasies from the same era, such as *Here Comes Mr. Jordan* and *It's a Wonderful Life*—considered a classic today—also failed.

*The Horn Blows at Midnight* did poorly at the box office, but it met with some favorable reviews. Jack's writers noticed that a line about the film drew a big laugh on the radio program, so they began peppering the scripts with references to the picture. For the sake of comedy, a cute and novel movie was made to become Jack's worst film. *The Horn Blows at Midnight* played briefly at Warner Brothers-owned theaters, then had to be revived due to the success of the humor Jack poked at it on his show.

For instance:

> JACK (to guard at Warner Brothers studio lot): Don't you recognize me? I'm Jack Benny. I made a movie here at Warner Brothers. *The Horn Blows at Midnight*. Didn't you see it?
> GUARD: See it? I directed it!

Or:

> TEENAGER: You know, Mr. Benny, you're so great. Why didn't you make any movies?
> DON WILSON: Oh, but he did. He made movies like *The Horn Blows*—
> JACK: Hold it, Don. Here's your autograph. Goodbye.
> DON: Jack, why didn't you let me tell him about *The Horn Blows at Midnight*?
> JACK: Just think, Don. Isn't it wonderful? A whole new generation that doesn't know.

*The Horn Blows at Midnight* (1945);
Lobby card (courtesy of Laura Leff)

Jack was never to star in another feature film, appearing only in cameos and walk-ons thereafter. He planned to revive his film career in the 1970s, signing to star in *The Sunshine Boys* with Walter Matthau, but pancreatic cancer took him in December of 1974. Jack's friend of many years, George Burns, came out of semi-retirement to make the film with Matthau. It won Burns an Oscar and revived his career.

Jack's film work peaked in the early 1940s. He once summed up the failure of his movie career by commenting, "When the horn blew at midnight, it blew taps for my film career."

But at the same time, his radio (and TV) work was about to take off for the stratosphere. The horn must have played reveille after it blew taps.

# Jack Benny and Fred Allen: The Fierce Fighting of Good Friends
### by Noell Wolfgram Evans

"Fred Allen was the best wit, the best extemporaneous comedian I ever knew."

—Jack Benny

"Jack Benny ought to be ashamed of himself."

—Fred Allen

## OLD FRIENDS

Fred Allen and Jack Benny became friends during their days in vaudeville. It may have been a case of opposites attracting—Allen with his quick, urbane, somewhat angry wit and Benny's calm, tightly scripted character comedy. The performers were on different ends of the comedy spectrum, but each was at the top of his game.

They developed a professional and personal friendship based on respect for each other's comic abilities, the irony being that each would later reap much personal, popular, and professional acclaim through verbally tearing those abilities apart. Though not immediately evident, their "feud" was built on admiration, affection, and comic possibilities.

## JUMPING MEDIUMS

Benny and Allen each made successful tours of vaudeville before moving to Broadway, where they were noticed by the developers of a new medium—radio. Benny moved to radio first, became an overnight sensation, and left for a radio career in sunny California.

Allen stayed behind in New York, building his program's popularity. Had he followed Benny to California, or had Benny stayed in New York, the feud would never have found its traction. The participants being a continent apart gave the feud its gravity, and a certain grandiosity that made it universal.

The feud became a running war of words and gags, volleyed across the airwaves (and later on the silver screen and through the cathode tubes of television). In our current age of pre-packaged media hype, the organic development of the Benny/Allen feud is most impressive. Benny once stated that he and Allen "never planned the feud, and if we had, it probably wouldn't have lasted more than a few broadcasts." In truth, though Benny may not have known, Allen manipulated the feud into place, kindled it into a blazing fire. After the feud was off and running, Allen implied that it had played out just as he had wanted. He started the duel with a jab at Benny, hoping his old friend would pick up on it and fire back on his next broadcast. Allen's rationale was based on simple math: Benny had a larger audience and Allen hoped that some back-and-forth between the two comedians would increase his audience size.

This is not to say that Benny was an unwitting accomplice. He was savvy enough to know that his audience would grow, too, with the added publicity. He understood the comic possibilities of locking horns with a regular adversary.

In the beginning, the feud was a feud in the literal sense of the word, but over time it evolved into something greater. It ceased being a pure fight and became more of a loose comic device that forever linked the two performers.

## LET THE BATTLE BEGIN

It all began on Fred Allen's program on December 30, 1936. That show featured Stuart Canin, a ten-year-old violin prodigy. After some idle banter with Allen, Canin played a rendition of Francois Schubert's "The Bee." At the completion of the song, Allen, in complimenting the young musician, made the comment: "Jack Benny should be ashamed of himself." And the war was on.

Allen's program aired on Wednesdays and Benny's on Sundays, so Benny had to wait to deliver a response. On his show of January 3, 1937, Benny addresses the issue. Toward the end of the show, he asks Mary to take a wire and dictates a note to Fred Allen, saying that he can too play "The Bee," accentuating his statement with a Bronx Cheer.

On his show three days later, Allen casts doubt on Benny's claim. The remark is made cautiously, as if Allen is feeling his way around the fight's parameters. On Benny's next show, the feud moves to a new level, becoming the main thrust of the program. Cast members ask Jack about Allen's comments, leading to long discussions which spread into the structure of the night's play. Interestingly, and completely within Benny's style of comedy, the cast doesn't attack Allen. They agree with him.

A few weeks of sniping go by until Benny attempts to put things to rest by playing "The Bee" on his show of February 7. At the climactic moment, however, Benny discovers his violin has been stolen. It's a brilliant piece of comedy and exactly what the feud needs. The audience has been drawn into the feud now and feels they're a part of it. The theft of the violin taking place at this point in the feud is a great example of Benny's comedic timing.

Sensing the rising public interest in the fight and realizing that Benny has raised the stakes, Allen goes full-out on his February 10 broadcast, featuring the showcase skit: "The Bennys Through History."

The feud spilled outside the confines of the two home shows. On February 15, 1937, Jack guest-starred on *Lux Radio Theatre.* In the discourse at the end of the show he managed this exchange with host Cecil B. DeMille:

> BENNY: While I'm here I'd be happy to play "The Bee."
> DEMILLE: That's an obsession that's gone to your head!

Benny let the feud fester before launching his next attack on February 28. Again, pitch-perfect timing. Allowing the feud to stew heightened audience anticipation. The Allen team, no comic slouches themselves, knew they had to wait; it was Benny's "turn." If Allen acted too quickly, the public might see him as a crank more than a comic. Benny plays "The Bee" on his February 28 program, and at the show's end smartly remarks, "Well, what now, Mr. Allen?"

Allen snipes back on his next show, but the feud's momentum has shifted to Benny. Feeling confident, Benny heads to New York for the inevitable showdown with Allen. While in New York, Benny pays a visit to Stuart Canin, the spark that ignited the feud/fuse. On Benny's March 7 broadcast, Canin greets Jack with: "If this is about the violin, I don't give lessons."

Next came what is referred to in boxing circles as "The Main Event." Benny and Allen were to meet for the first time since the feud began. The event took place on Benny's show of March 14, from the St. Pierre Ballroom in New York City. The room buzzes with electricity, an excitement the likes of which is usually reserved for the seventh game of the World Series. The two old pros do not disappoint.

Back and forth they go in a volley of escalating anger, until physicality is the only possible outcome. Still verbally sparring, Benny and Allen storm out to the hallway to settle matters once and for all. After a tense minute, wherein Benny's cast discuss his fate, Benny and Allen return arm in arm, swapping stories and giggling like schoolgirls. Mary's remark as to Jack's black eye is brushed off as Benny continues his love-fest with Allen. Anti-climactic? Perhaps, but the audience ate it up; the broadcast was the highest rated program of 1937.

The feud eventually flared up again and ran for almost twenty years, lessening in prominence at times, seemingly running out of steam here and there. Each comedian, however, found ways to breathe new life into what became a masterpiece of comedy.

Some highlights and milestones:

* On March 24, 1940, Jack appeared as a guest on *The Campbell Playhouse.* His character took part in the following conversation:
  "One guy I never miss…fellow by the name of Jack Benny."
  "Jack Benny? Sure I hear about him all the time on *The Fred Allen Show.*"
* The boys put aside their differences when they appeared at the tail end of the 1942 Christmas Eve broadcast of *Command Performance.* Benny and Allen banter a bit, and then sing the Cole Porter song "Friendship." They end up using the song as a way to "sweetly" hurl insults at one another.
* In October of 1945, Fred Allen moved his show from CBS to NBC. He was given a Sunday night timeslot, just a half hour after Benny's show, putting Benny and Allen on top of each other and making the feud practically unavoidable.
* In 1948, in the midst of minor ratings slides for both programs, Allen and Benny spent five weeks of consecutive shows (April 11 through May 9)

hitting each other with blistering attacks. The skillful staging reinvigorated the comedians and revived the public interest in the feud.

* June 26, 1949 marked the end of Allen's weekly program. Benny's show of May 22, 1955 was his last on radio. The men had often been featured guest stars on each other's programs, the appearances crackling with the back-story of the feud, the anticipation of insults forever heightening the proceedings.

## GANGING UP ON JACK

Since Benny's show topped the charts before Stuart Canin put his bow to the strings, Allen was the main ratings beneficiary of the feud. But in 1945, Jack's show hit a slump, dropping him out of the top five. The Benny staff was concerned but not desperate. They knew Jack was still Jack and people loved him, but something had to be done to increase interest in the show. So the writers combined two of Benny's strengths: his program's clever tweaking of commercial ploys and the feud with Allen. Listeners were asked to compose a 25-word essay with the title "I Can't Stand Jack Benny Because..."

Using impeccable logic, Benny hired Fred Allen to be the honorary judge of the contest. Fred relished the position, though he found himself on the receiving end of an entry or two, as in: "I Can't Stand Jack Benny Because...he built up Fred Allen and him I can't stand."

## THOSE ARE FIGHTING WORDS!

Allen constantly attacked the Benny-isms of cheapness and age. On the other hand, Benny's favorite target was Allen's poor physical condition.

*ALLEN (after hearing that Benny had been nominated to open the March of Dimes drive): "The dime hasn't been minted that could march past Jack."

*BENNY: "Listening to Fred Allen is like listening to two Abbotts and no Costello."

*ALLEN: "He's been playing the violin for thirty years and still has trouble getting it out of the case."

*BENNY: "With those bags under his eyes he looks like a short butcher peering over two pounds of liver."

*ALLEN: "The only time Benny ever left a tip was when he couldn't finish his asparagus."

*BENNY: "Fred Allen is so tight, when he finally spends a five-dollar bill, Lincoln's eyes are bloodshot."

*ALLEN: "Benny looks like he just got down to give his pallbearers' shoulders a rest."

## FEUDING ON A FORTY-FOOT SCREEN

In 1940 Benny and Allen took their feud to the big screen with the film *Love Thy Neighbor*. It didn't work. On radio the feud was parsed out in pieces, between shows, over weeks. Compacted as it was in the movie, the feud came off as angry and scripted, not playful and free flowing.

A major weakness of the film is Benny's immediate taking and keeping of the upper hand (that is, until the great gag at the end). On their radio shows, Allen always seemed to be one step ahead of Jack. In *Love Thy Neighbor,* Allen was the one with the nervous edge while Jack played the more aggressive role. The identity switch didn't play well.

In a rare moment of mutual agreement and harmony, at the premier of *Love Thy Neighbor* Benny and Allen presented Stuart Canin with a check for a thousand dollars, which he put toward his music education. Canin went on to become an accomplished concertmaster.

In 1945 Benny and Allen appeared in a second film—*It's in the Bag*—which tells a more cohesive story, interweaving the feud only when appropriate. Allen plays Fred F. Trumble Floogle, the heir to a pile of money. The cash, however, is hidden in one of five chairs he has just given away. Benny, appearing as himself, has purchased one of the chairs.

Their scenes together are short but memorable. Here, Allen's character poses as the president of a chapter of the Jack Benny Fan Club, telling Benny that turnout has been poor for his latest film.

> BENNY: Have you tried giving away dishes?
> ALLEN: Yes, and they ended up throwing them at the screen.
> BENNY: Well, have you tried not giving out dishes?
> ALLEN: Yes, and they just went and brought them from home.

Allen's *voice* made a cameo in 1940's *Buck Benny Rides Again*, but *Love They Neighbor* and *It's in the Bag* marked Benny and Allen's only big screen face-offs.

## THE MAGIC OF TELEVISION

Benny was one of the last radio stars to make the transition to television. The wait didn't hurt him, as his show was an immediate hit. Allen, sadly, wasn't able to make a successful leap to the new medium, his time there relegated to one-shots and guest-starring roles.

In their only TV appearance together, Allen guest-starred on Benny's show of April 19, 1953. Benny visits his sponsor. Unbeknownst to him, Allen is there too, looking to take over Jack's job. The show is quick and funny. Television seemed to add a jolt of life to the old feud. It's a shame the two weren't paired together more often.

## AFTERMATH

The advent of television and the changing tastes of the audience led to the decline of Fred Allen's career in show business. His acerbic comedy style fell out of favor, and although he found sporadic work on TV and did lots of writing, he failed to regain the attention and acclaim he once held.

Fred died on March 17, 1955. For a man inexorably linked to the current events of the day, it was fitting for Fred to die of a heart attack on a New York sidewalk while on his way to buy a newspaper.

Jack broke down when he heard the news of Fred's death. He was honored to be asked to deliver Fred's eulogy. A sweet and fitting tribute for two men so connected.

Jack had relished the feud. It provided him with brilliant comic material, gave him the chance to perform with a friend, and helped to boost his popularity. Perhaps best of all for Jack, it gave him the chance to watch Allen at work.

"Fred was brilliant and had a much more difficult time with the feud than I did. I had a whole week after his show to plan my retorts, but Fred had only a half hour from the time I finished my program before he went on the air with a completely written and rehearsed show. And yet he managed to come up with hilarious gags in answer to me right after I'd finish...and he did it consistently, week after week after week."

Jack Benny and Fred Allen. Two men linked together. A team that wasn't a team, though one could argue that they were. Since Allen's passing, no two performers have found the mix of love, anger, admiration, discontent, and respect that Allen and Benny had. Two entertainers with fans around the world, yet they seemed to be performing only for each other. We can be thankful they chose to have their private laughs on such a public stage.

# JACK BENNY—TENTH YEAR IN RADIO

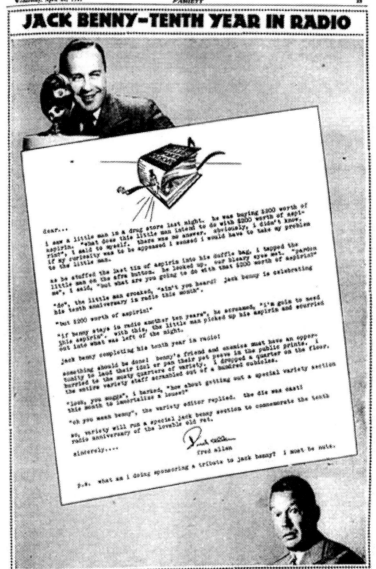

(Kathryn Fuller-Seeley collection)

# My Adventures in Hollywood

## by Jack Benny

(from *Radio Stars* magazine, November, 1935, Ben Ohmart collection)

Good evening, folks.

These movie people have quite a town out here. A big town and a little town, a good town and a bad town, a wise town and a dumb town all rolled into one. I like it. I like it, if you want a reason, because you can't be lonesome, and in that respect, Hollywood stands all alone and at the head of the class. I like it because up to now it has been pretty darned good to this son of radio. And I like Hollywood, too, because Mary likes it.

Somebody called this place the world's grab-bag; you stick in your hand and get a surprise package that you'll get nowhere else on earth.

For instance, where else can you find bills-of-fare with such knee-high prices? Honestly, one of the first things I noticed was that a ten-dollar dinner on Broadway came to about two Hollywood dollars. Think what that does to a guy whose self-esteem is tied to his pocketbook.

Sardi's is one of those places. You can get more to eat there for ninety cents than anywhere west of the Bowery soup kitchens. It's a buffet luncheon where you take whatever you want. Eight or a dozen meats, as many salads, desserts, coffee, tea.

Or if you're in a twenty-cent mood you can roll your car up to one of the huge drive-in sandwicheries that the boys have built on almost every other corner. Those drive-in places really have to be seen to be believed. If ever you're a tourist in Southern California, try it yourself. It's an emotional as well as a gastronomical experience.

You're rolling along Wilshire Boulevard, for instance, when the pangs of hunger hit you. Over on the right is a structure that looks like a cross between the Ford building at the World's Fair and a merry-go-round. Usually, it is painted blue or yellow or scarlet...Something easy on the eyes—if you're wearing dark glasses.

You roll your car into an opening between a Buick from Missouri and a Chrysler from Milwaukee. From the air, these places must look like a lot of wheels, with the cars forming the spokes of the wheel and the sandwichery the hub.

You've just had time to switch off your ignition when a Follies dolly in blue and white gingham floats up and takes your order. Inside three deep breaths of this wonderful sunshine-washed California air, she's back fastening a tray to your car-side and filling it with a culinary creation that would delight even Primo Carnera. All for twenty cents. Yeah, as I was saying, I like this town.

Of course, if you've money to spend and the formal clothes to spend it in, the Troc's the place to go. Troc is short for Trocadero, which is the place to see and be seen in your best big and tucker. Mary and I tried and found as fine a midnight supper and show as New York or Chicago can offer. Maybe you read about that time Garbo went stepping and ran into Dietrich and cut her dead. That happened there, and I'd give one of [Don] Bestor's spats to have seen it.

Probably you already know about the Brown Derby; it's got a lot of booths and mostly the male stars eat there. And the Vendome with its knotty pine tables. Just a low building on Sunset Boulevard, but if you're ever within a thousand miles, there's one thing you oughtn't to miss. It is the girl behind the cigar counter.

That girl—I don't even know her name—is one of the prettiest things I've seen outside the storybooks. Not one star out of ten can match her for looks, yet she is selling cigars. Why? Why isn't she making movies? You ask yourself that question often, as you walk around this town. Beauty is all over the place, selling sandwiches, cigars, waiting on tables. Kids burning with ambition, waiting for their chance in the flickers. They'll get it someday, and then they'll either click big or go back to some decent guy who'd rather have plain Jane Doe for his honey than a Marlene or a Jean.

One of the crazy things that happen to you out here is *people*. In radio, you know, you go to the studio the day of your broadcast and rehearse for a few hours. That night you put on a show and then go back home. Maybe, during the dozen hours you are about, you see some people you know. Afterwards, you don't see anyone but strangers or friends from some other field.

Hollywood is different. You eat movies, sleep movies, smell movies. I think it is because the town is small and you're continually rubbing elbows with folks you know almost well enough to kid. And let me tell you, you can't rub elbows with some of them without something happening to you.

Garbo, for instance. She reminds me of Jessica Dragonette. Jessica has lots of natural beauty and with her new haircut she's prettier than ever, but the thing you feel about her is the mental force she puts into her job. She says a little prayer every time she sings, you know. And something more than her voice goes through the mike, just as something more than Garbo's external appearance goes through the camera lens. Jessica is in pictures now, too. I wish Garbo were on the radio. That link between them—that depth—would be interesting to observe.

Jean Harlow walks on to your set. She talks about books and philosophy and whether horseracing is a good or bad influence. You find she's one of the best-read women you've met. She has life all worked out. Live for today! Forget tomorrow. It may never come. The past has gone. Why worry? Today is here. Let it do its best for you. And after ten minutes talking to Jean you are ready to launch a thousand ships.

As for Myrna Loy. Now there is a woman a man can never forget. She has a knack which gives a man an entirely new thought about a woman. *She can listen.* She leans slightly forward, a lithe, bright-eyed hollyhock, swaying slightly in a light breeze. Her eyes are stars twinkling approval. Her lips part slightly like delicate petals awaiting rain. And *your* words are that rain. I guess I'm going poetic. But that's what Myrna Loy does even to a Benny.

Myrna doesn't make a man feel like just an extra in life. He's the whole show. He's the star from the first moment he sits down with her until she says she must go, not with words but by gathering her hankie and bag and smiling the loveliest farewell you've ever had said to you.

Of course, when you've met these women and come to know them, you remember radio. And you wish they were on your program. They'd bring the pulsating vigor of youth to the loudspeaker. Don't ask me how, but they'd do it—and it's something radio could use.

As for Myrna, she's got a standing offer to join my hour. And she won't need to say a word. She can just sit there in the first row of the audience, where each of us can see her. We'll broadcast to her, in person. She'll make us so good, just by the way she listens, that we'll be better than our best.

Now, here's a thing about this town I like, too. People have cut out the false modesty. And it's wonderful, I mean it. Most places, people talk about ego and conceit as if they were diseases. Well, I've still got to meet the guy who makes the other fellow believe in him unless he believes in himself. Take a kid. If he wins the high jump, he's proud and happy about it. He doesn't hide the fact he's done something big by saying: "Someone else took that jump for me." He knows he did it and he went a little higher than the other fellow.

Somehow, outside of Hollywood, a man who's succeeded in *his* jump is supposed to act as though he didn't know he'd been jumping. He's supposed to show the world a face blushing from modesty when it should properly blush from pride.

In Hollywood, they're honest. Here they don't brag about things they haven't done, but they are enthusiastic and bubbling over from excitement about what they have accomplished. If Lupe Velez has just signed a contract for big money in South America, she tells you about it. She tells you the salary, tells what a new fame in a new land is going to mean to her. She's a kid who's won another race and she wants everyone to enjoy the fact with her.

Why, these folks out here like the way they act so well they play charades at private parties. They show each other their latest films, their newest publicity pictures. They have photographs of themselves sitting possessively on grand pianos. They are stars. They are important. They know it. And they expect and want you to know it.

Yeah, it's a crazy town, and a grand town. I could go on for another ten million words about it. Hollywood, like a Hollywood party, never stops. Which reminds me, the other night Mary and I threw a pretty sizable party for Fred Allen and Portland Hoffa. It was the first week of their stay out here and I wanted them to meet all the right people.

I was receiving the guests at my front door. One fellow I'd known around New York in the old days but hadn't met for some time saw me standing there. He came over and stuck his hand up. "Jack Benny! Of all people. What are *you* doing here?"

He didn't realize he'd come to my party. And that's typical of Hollywood.

P.S. I just read this over. I made an awful *faux pas*. I forgot to mention the name of the picture I came out here to make. It's *Broadway Melody of 1936*.

# Benny's Floopers and Blubs
## (Uh, Bloopers and Flubs)

### by Michael Leannah

They say it's impolite to laugh at other people's mistakes, but for listeners of Jack Benny's radio show, nothing gave more delight than laughing at the cast's frequent bloopers and flubs.

Not to diminish the work of the show's talented writers, but the greatest laughs the show produced came about by accident: misread lines and the subsequent attempts to save face through clever ad-libs. One indicator of the depth of talent among the Benny show's cast was their ability to ad-lib their way out of difficult situations.

Early in the show's history, flubs were few and far between, politely sidestepped and ignored. It took time for the flub to evolve into a subcategory of the humor itself. Early on, a spate of bloopers would have possibly brought on the show's demise. Benny had difficulty retaining a sponsor in the beginning. If his show was seen as slipshod and disorganized, the task of getting and keeping a sponsor would have been all the more difficult. And, to be sure, individuals had to be mindful of the dangers of flubbing too frequently. Had Don or Phil, for instance, stumbled often in their initial assignments, they would have been promptly replaced.

But Jack Benny was a brave one. He brought on the wrath of sponsors by purposefully denigrating the products during comical commercials, which didn't go over well with the stuffed shirts at the top. In a similar way, Jack came to relish the mistakes made by his cast. A different entertainer would have been chagrined at frequent bloopers, but Jack saw them as part of the fun, an opportunity to scramble for an ad-lib, a chance to capitalize on the serendipitous.

Jack pounced on the mistakes of others. Mary and Don made the most missteps and neither was very astute at covering their tracks, usually laughing through a second attempt of the broken line. Jack was often able to catch himself in a flub and make the most of it. Phil Harris held his own. Rochester and Dennis also occasionally demonstrated the ability to think on their feet. And the audience loved to laugh along.

A discerning ear can detect a separate quality to the laughter brought on by a flub, as opposed to that produced by a planned joke. This is true for laughter from members of the cast as well as from the audience. For instance, Don Wilson's familiar chortle accompanies almost all of the gags on the show. When a flub occurs, a sense of surprise can be heard in his laugh.

Flubs on *The Jack Benny Program* evolved to the point where there was no shame or embarrassment, no attempt to gloss over or cover up the mistakes, as evidenced by this exchange from October 26, 1952, when Bob Crosby was new to the program:

> BOB (inspecting Jack's swimming pool): I've been thinking about have— put—I've been thinking of having one put in myself.
> (Audience laughter)
> JACK: Don't worry about it, Bob. We've been doing that for years.

With the typical flub, audience laughter erupts after each new piece of the puzzle is joined. Jack feigns anger and makes it sound as if no one seems to think rehearsals are needed. "All I ask is one rehearsal!" is a common lament after a blooper.

The regular cast—Jack, Mary, Phil, Rochester, Don, and Dennis—all made their share of flubs, as did guest stars and those in the peripheral cast. Jack knew that the flow of a show could be broken by impulsively jumping on a miscue. He had an uncanny sense for when to jump and when to pass. A miscue, if handled correctly, could be milked for laughs for weeks. Some of the bloopers on the Benny show remain for many listeners the show's most memorable moments.

Often, the bloopers weren't funny by themselves. It was the reactions of Jack and the other cast members that made them hilarious. The audience loved to hear Jack tease Mary when she turned a line into a Spoonerism or stumbled her way through a difficult line. And they heartily enjoyed it when Jack blustered angrily at Phil for stumbling on a multisyllabic word, only to have Phil prattle back with a smart-aleck retort.

The heyday for flubs on Benny's show was from 1945 through 1951. Pick a show at random and you're almost certain to hear one. Or three or four. They were an integral part of the show. Benny's format lent itself to the interplay the bloopers created. Mistakes on lesser shows made the actors appear unskilled or amateurish. Not so with Benny. He might have been called a "Teflon" comedian.

If mistakes were so well received by the audience, why then didn't the writers simply write them in? From time to time Jack's writers did write bloopers into the script, but only as a means of portraying a character's excitement or anxiety, as when Jack, about to receive a visit from his sponsor, said to Don Wilson, "Sit Don, Down. I mean, sit down, Don." The audience knew this was a scripted mistake; it garnered a mere chuckle.

The kind of bloopers that brought the house down could not have been written into the script. In Chuck Schaden's book, *Speaking of Radio*, Phil Harris is quoted: "There's no way you can fix a flub. No way! They have tried every way in the world. You can't set one up." Phil admitted that at times when a hilarious flub was made in the first show (for the East Coast), the writers were tempted to write it into the second (West Coast) show, but they always decided against it. "It won't play…As far as settin' a trap, it won't work."

There was no rule that said the writers couldn't rig things in their favor, however. Witness this piece from May 1, 1949, in which Phil stumbles on the word "dynomometer":

> PHIL: Be sure you get one of those new models that comes with the multi-coil hydro-tension duo-vacuum dyno-mahter...

Phil is interrupted by laughter from the audience, then recovers well:
"They come in a mahter and a fahter mahter."

It couldn't have been easy to breeze through every script without incident. Most people experience stage fright to some degree. Even when not reading into a microphone feeding broadcast stations transmitting coast to coast, people make mistakes when reading aloud. Dennis admitted late in life to being so nervous on the show that seasoned actress Verna Felton was brought on as his mother to act as a buffer for him.

The types of bloopers on Jack Benny's show ran the gamut, from timing problems—someone answering a phone before it rings or opening a door before a visitor knocks—to stutterings and Spoonerisms.

A good example of a timing flub occurred on the show of May 9, 1948. Benny is telling his version of what happened when he was robbed of the Oscar he had borrowed from his neighbor, Ronald Colman. He claims he was giving the robbers a thorough beating when one of them called for the use of a "rocket bomb."

> ROBBER: This guy's a tough one. We'll have to use our last resort. Give it to him!
> (Long empty pause, followed by a prolonged blast.)
> BENNY: Ohhhh. It was a long time coming, but ohhhh.

Hard to imagine the scene getting anywhere near the amount of laughter had it been read without incident.

Another timing mistake took place in the show of February 8, 1953, in which Jack takes the gang for a steak ride in Palm Springs.

> JACK: Come on, everybody, we'll get our horses. Over here, Don! Bob!
> (Long pause.)
> BOB: We're with you, Jack.
> JACK: I didn't think you *were* there for a minute.

Spoonerisms occur when the initial sounds of two or more words are transposed, creating a comic effect (as in the title of this chapter). Benny's shows are littered with flubs of this type, as well as ones made when whole words are switched, such as when Rochester, on November 22, 1942, said while trying to lift Benny's sway-backed horse up off the ground, "Here's the boss, Jack—uh, here's the jack, boss."

These mistakes often led to bits that ran for weeks. In 1945, Phil mangled a line by switching the word "Vermont" with "vermouth." A couple of weeks later, Jack says in an exasperated aside, "Phil, take your vermouth and go to Vermont."

Mary was responsible for a strange script switcheroo when she chided Jack for wearing a white suit to the Easter parade on April 5, 1953:

> MARY: Well, if you're going to wear it, wipe that tomato soup satin off the lapel. Stain!
> JACK: Tomato soup what?...I've heard everything now....Wipe that tomato soup satin? From a distance it looks like a red carnation.

Later in the same broadcast, the writers rework the script so Bob Crosby can refer to his former sponsor, Campbell Soup, as "Y'know, the outfit that made your carnation."

The errors themselves made for hilarious comedy, but the audience seemed to have a special appreciation for the quick ad-lib after the flub. Jack was especially adept at recovering a busted script with an appropriate rejoinder. This from March 24, 1946:

> MARY: Oh, Jack. You always hate the movies this time of year because you never win the Academy Award.
> JACK: Mary, that has nothing to do with it. Comedy pictures get very little consideration. I've found out one thing. To win an Academy Award you've got to do a picture with absolutely no laughter.
> MARY: Well, your darn one last near made it.

After much laughter, Jack confides in the audience with, "I think you got the idea." Then, to Mary: "I don't mind when you foul up a lousy gag, but that was such a good one."

On the program of November 12, 1950, Don gives Jack a golden opportunity to think on his feet by flubbing the initial introduction after the theme music faded:

> DON: Ladies and Gentlemen, it's evening at the Benny household. Rochester has just finished—uh, Jack has just finished dinner and now is in the kitchen helping Rochester with the dishes.
> JACK: Did you enjoy your dinner, Rochester?

Phil was no slouch in the quick recovery department either; he could go toe-to-toe with the ad-libbing Benny. On the show of June 27, 1948 Phil says he was in Philadelphia for the Republican convention.

> PHIL: I was chairman of the delegadation from Doo-Wah-Diddy.
> JACK (over audience laughter): You can't give him those words!
> PHIL: Well, why do you keep puttin' 'em in there?

Benny, at times, was a bit subtle in the way he poked fun. Take this example from November 6, 1949, in which Rochester tries to explain to his boss why the price of coffee was so high:

> ROCHESTER: Well, Mr. Benny, it's simple. In school I studied international eco-economics.
> JACK: In school?
> ROCHESTER: Yup. Now, ah—
> JACK: In school I learned how to pronounce "economics".

A similar example is found in the broadcast of September 24, 1950:

> MAN FROM CALABASAS: Heard your show last week. Laughed so hard I fell off my milkin' stool.
> JACK: Now, look—
> MAN: Now if it hadn't been—if I hadn't had a good grip on that cow, I'd have broke my nose.
> JACK: If you hadn't muffed that line you'd have gotten a bigger laugh, too.

Guest stars from Frank Sinatra to Jimmy Stewart made flubs on Benny's show. Perhaps the funniest mistakes were made by guests who normally didn't find themselves in front of a mike. Producer Darryl Zanuck botched the title of Jack's song, calling it "When I Say I Beg Your Pardon, Then I'll Come Back to You."

Not to be outdone, Jack Warner appeared on the program of February 20, 1949. Hardly a smooth performer, Warner banters stiffly with Jack, trying to convince him to refrain from resurrecting *The Horn Blows at Midnight* for a Ford Theater performance.

> WARNER: We spent over five hundred thousand dollars for a new finish and nobody even—ever—stayed to see it.
> JACK: No wonder you can't make good pictures. You fluff over lines and...

Later, Warner offers money to Jack if he'll agree to not do the show. Benny says money means nothing to him.

> MARY: I've got to listen to the repeat show and see if he really heard that.
> JACK: See if *I* really heard that. You oughta make pictures with Jack Warner. I know we rehearsed this!

Warner becomes unnerved and twice loses his place in the script, causing an audience uproar.

> JACK: I could get a fifty-dollar actor to play Jack Warner. I had to get *the* Jack Warner.

Occasionally Jack even worked laughs from correctly-read lines. On March 16, 1947, Mary delivered a long difficult passage without the slightest trouble. Jack responded with, "Hey, that was a long speech and you got it out. I'm always worried about those long speeches."

Mary's mistakes were often made in a tentative manner. Jack had to stop and wonder, "Did she really say that?" Not so with poor Don Wilson. With his booming announcer's voice, there was never a doubt:

> "Jack, Jack! You and better Mary—uh, you and Mary better get on stage."

The best of the bloopers gave fodder to the writers for gags drawn out for weeks or even months. On the show of October 27, 1946, Jack and Mary are in a diner and Mary asks for a "Chiss sweeze sandwich." The following week Mary can't find her lipstick. Don suggests she turn her purse upside-down and empty it. When she does, the listeners are treated to a classic sound effect—one that TV wouldn't be able to recreate—of a dump truck unloading its contents for several seconds. Jack finally says, "Mary, empty the rest of it in the hall. This room's filled already. What a lot of junk! And look, three Chiss sweeze sandwiches."

Later in the same broadcast:

> MARY: Polly want a cracker?
> POLLY: Polly want a Chiss sweeze sandwich.

Edward G. Robinson appeared on the show of November 24, 1946, playing the part of a tough guy swaggering into a restaurant run by Benny. When Robinson takes too long to order, Benny tells him to hurry up or he'll call the police.

> ROBINSON: One move out of you and I'll fill you so full of holes you'll look like a Chiss sweeze sandwich.
> BENNY: That's Swiss cheese.
> ROBINSON: Don't tell me how to get a laugh.

The audience loved each new reference to the original flub.

Another blooper that became a goldmine for the writers was the famous "Dreer Poosen"—Don Wilson's mangling of "Drew Pearson." In fact, the show on which the initial mistake was made (January 8, 1950) was the mother lode for flub-lovers.

> JACK: Don, how did you know I bought a new suit?
> DON: I heard it on Dreer Poos—.
> JACK: You heard it on what? Wait a minute. I want to hear this. You heard it on what?
> DON: I heard it on Drew Pearson's broadcast.
> JACK: Ladies and Gentlemen, he got the award for being the best announcer! That gives you a rough idea.

Don, Mary, Jack, Dennis

On the same show, during the "Murder at Romanoff's" sketch, Mary says, "Carlton Quince was quilled—killed!" The Sportsmen Quartet starts and stops through a short musical break, apparently unsure of their script assignment, causing Jack to erupt with: "That was the lousiest thing I ever heard in my life!" And, famously, near the show's end the writers surprise Jack by changing Frank Nelson's line. The response to "Pardon me, are you the doorman?" was supposed to be: "Well, who do think I am wearing this red uniform, Nelson Eddy?" Benny cracked up on the set when instead he was treated with: "Well, who do you think I am, Dreer Poosen?"

The Dreer Poosen jokes ran for weeks. On January 15, 1950, Rochester is making out the weekly payroll for the cast:

> JACK: On Don Wilson's check, deduct fifty cents.
> ROCHESTER: Fifty cents?
> JACK: Yes, and on the stub make a notation: Deduction for D.P.
> ROCHESTER: D.P.? What does that stand for?
> JACK: Dreer Poosen. He'll understand.

Scanning books in his library, Jack says, "Here's one. *My Ten Years in Washington* by Dreer Poosen. Well, I'll be darned. There is a Dreer Poosen. I hope Don doesn't find out."

Another flub that turned into a running joke began on December 3, 1950, when Mary turned the term "grease rack" into "grass reek." Since the miscue happened at the very end of the program, further jokes had to wait until the following week. Don Wilson got things off with a bang when he objected to Jack complaining about Mary's mistake.

> DON: Jack, you're not pushing Mary for that little mistake she made on last week's program.
> JACK: "Pushing?" That's "punishing." Nobody *reads* on this program.

Jack banishes Mary from the stage, making her repeat "grease rack" fifty times. (Jack later used this tactic again when Don misspoke and said, "Be Lucky, Go Happy" while reading a commercial for Lucky Strike cigarettes.) The Chief of Police of Palm Springs makes an appearance and describes some trouble he had with a skunk on the lawn. "Boy, did that grass reek!" he says. Later, Mary relates the story of the skunk.

> MARY: Boy, did that grease rack!
> JACK: That's grass reek.
> MARY: Well, make up your mind!

Flubs and bloopers were the topic of the program on May 8, 1949. The show opens with Jack criticizing the cast for mistakes made the previous week, "one of the sloppiest shows I've ever heard. Everyone flubbing their lines, missing their cues." He scolds Mary for stuttering through a letter from her mother. "I haven't heard you get words so mixed up since that time in the restaurant you ordered a Chiss sweeze sandwich."

Phil Harris is the next to feel the wrath of Benny. "Phil, you were supposed to say multi-coil hydro-tension duo-vacuum dyno-mometer. Instead of that you said multi-coil hydro-tension duo-vacuum dyno-momayter." Phil responds with: "And I stayed on the wagon all week to get that line right."

Later, in a diner, Mary orders a Chiss sweeze sandwich. Jack's scolding is interrupted by the clerk (Frank Nelson) who says they make wonderful Chiss sweeze sandwiches there. Jack says, "You do? Then I'll try a Chiss sweeze sandwich." Nelson lets him have it: "Would you like me to crim the trusts?"

Of all the cast members, Mary Livingstone got the prize for making the most on-air flubs. Was her notorious mike-fright to blame? Or was it simply a lack of concentration?

> MARY (discussing why Jack wasn't chosen for the role of Jesse James): 'Cause every time they shot a gun his toupee blew off.
> JACK: Mary, that wasn't a toupee. That was my mask that blew off.
> MARY: Since—uh—since when does a mask have Bobby's pins?
> JACK: Bobby's pins?
> MARY: Bobby's pins?
> JACK: Bobby's pins? Mary, that's bobby pins, not Bobby's pins. They don't belong to Bobby, you know what I mean? (February 18, 1945)

JACK: You know, Mary, I wish Phil wouldn't keep talking about what a hit he was at the Palladium in London. Why can't he be modest about it, like me?

MARY: You? Modest?

JACK: Yes, me.

MARY: I've got ten answers for that one, any one will which will send me back to the May Company.

JACK: You miss a few more lines and you will go back to the May Company. (October 3, 1948)

MARY: But, Jack, you're a man. You shouldn't have worn the trunks. Why did you wear the trunks?

JACK: Read that right. Read that right.

MARY: Oh, I'm sorry.

(The audience laughs with her, then applauds.)

JACK: We'll never get off the air tonight.

MARY: But, Jack—

JACK: Yeah.

MARY:—you're a man—

JACK: Yeah.

MARY:—you should have just worn the trunks. Why did you wear the top? (March 26, 1950)

Eddie "Rochester" Anderson

Rochester took his turn now and then in the blooper parade and when he did he often garbled his lines so thoroughly they defy spelling. The show of February 20, 1944 opens with Rochester talking to himself as he cleans the library.

"This room certainly looks empty. Just a pair of bookends holding up a social-see-see-sue-social security card." The audience bursts into laughter, but since Rochester is supposedly alone in the room, no one in the cast can make more of it. He continues with his lines as if nothing happened. This flub, by the way, ought to put to rest any notion that mistakes were planned and practiced for the laughs they'd produce. Try saying "social security" the way Rochester did. It's downright impossible. Rochester himself couldn't have said it a second time if he'd tried. (Mary Livingstone, incidentally, had her own wrestling match with the phrase "social security" on the show of December 2, 1945.)

Phil Harris's forte where flubs were concerned was in butchering multisyllabic words not in his usual vocabulary.

> PHIL (at the completion of a song at rehearsal): Hey, fellas, when we do the number on the show, play it a little more pitz—ah—ah—pistachio.
> JACK: That's pizzicato! Pistachio! When we *give* you the wrong word you can't pronounce it. (April 25, 1948)

Jack himself was fairly immune from razzing when he committed mistakes. Phil or Mary jumped on him occasionally, but the others doing so would have been out of character. Still, Jack did make mistakes. Often he'd correct himself with his impeccable timing, much to the audience's delight.

While lecturing Dennis during the broadcast of March 14, 1948, Jack read the following with great emotion: "I'd get up at four o'clock in the morning on a cold wintry day. Pack my own lunch and trudge twelve miles through the snow, looking for work...And at night, with the pennies I had earned clunched in my little fist—clenched in my little fist, I would drag my weary body home..."

On the program of September 28, 1952, during the "High Noon" sketch, Jack botched his line. He tried to continue but with each additional line, the laughter increased, reaching a crescendo with Dennis Day's final punch line:

> JACK: I'm in trouble, Frank...I'm in trouble. Frank Miller's comin' back to town to kill me...I need help...Also, a rehearsal.
> DENNIS: You sure do.

Jack Benny was a pioneer in the world of comedy, a chance-taker, a rule-breaker. Not laugh at others' mistakes? Benny wouldn't hear of such nonsense. He thrived on it.

NBC promotional caricature of Dennis Day. Artist unknown

# Better Play, Don

## by Jack Benny

(from *Radio Guide* magazine, March 30, 1935, Ben Ohmart collection)

So you'd like to change places with me?

Well—there were a couple of times at the Chicago Theater when I'd gladly have traded with you. Particularly on Sunday, blessed Sabbath day on which you were reading in your family Bibles that Sunday was ordained as a day of rest.

What a rest! Three more Sundays like that one and you'd all be getting a rest—from Jack Benny at least. And we'd probably be resting in some nicely upholstered cells—or, if not resting, pacing around them proclaiming to other disillusioned inmates that we were the original Marathon runners.

The twenty-four preceding hours had set the stage for the most hectic day in our radio careers. We had played six exhausting shows on Saturday and dropped into bed at midnight too tired even to eat—and then came the dawn.

At nine in the morning we were in the studios of the National Broadcasting Company to rehearse our program for the evening. My voice was shot. (Frank) Parker's pipes needed a plumber and poor Mary had circles under her eyes that looked like the aftermath of a domestic tangle. It was 11 o'clock in the morning before we whipped the show into the semblance of presentability—and staring us in the face was a stage performance across the Loop at 11:40.

There was make-up to don—and Don to make up with, after the edginess of the rehearsal—but we accomplished it with about a half-minute to spare. Darn that Maestro Bestor, anyway! (Don Bestor was the orchestra leader on Benny's radio show from 1934 to 1935.) A combination luncheon and breakfast followed the first performance, and three more shows followed almost on one another's heels.

The fact that Sunday is a day of rest wasn't borne in on us until just before the time for our first broadcast. We luxuriated in repose for the ten minutes it takes to reach the Merchandise Mart in a cab. And Parker would insist on a series of *mimimis* all the way over. Some day I'm going to have trouble with that guy. He owes me a hundred bucks, by the way, but he'll probably pay that back promptly so he can touch me for two hundred soon after. He ought to be in the movies—but he'd probably prefer the stills—you know how it is—*mash* notes and everything.

After the first broadcast it was another Sir Malcolm Campbell dash back to the Chicago Theater for two more shows and over to the studios again for our last broadcast. That was the final straw for Mary—she managed to remain upright during the program, but fainted just as Bestor was playing the last number.

She wasn't able to appear in the first three stage shows on Monday which, off hand, may seem just like a circumstance but it meant revamping lines for everybody, providing new cues, and writing her out of the act temporarily. Swell girl, Mary; but there are times when she just can't take it!

But there's always Thursday—you know—when the auditor's representative comes back with the checks. Mary can take it then. In fact she takes it before I get a chance to look at it. But after a day like that Sunday, she earns it.

So you'd like to trade places with me?

O.K.; but make it any day but Thursday. Please change with Parker on Thursday—but not until he's paid me that hundred.

Sheet music featuring Jack Benny's early bandleader, Don Bestor.
From the Derek Tague collection.

# Jack and Johnny:
# To Each a Fan, To Each a Friend

## by Steve Newvine

Jack Benny's fan base extended to the baby boom generation in a big way. Many of us became fans as we watched the final years of his weekly TV show in the mid-1960s, or his annual specials during his "comedian emeritus" career stage in the late '60s and early '70s. As a young boy growing up in Port Leyden, New York, during those years, I became a Jack Benny fan because of Jack's relationship with Johnny Carson.

When Jack's TV show moved from early Sunday evening to a later time on Tuesday night, my viewing was compromised by parents who adhered to a strict school night bedtime schedule. So I got my Benny fixes through his guest appearances on other stars' programs or by watching his show during school vacations. Thankfully, the final season of Benny's program was broadcast on Friday nights. Thereafter, I enjoyed Jack's specials. And I became aware of another comedian who was making a name for himself in late-night television.

I convinced my mother to let me stay up late on Friday nights to watch *The Tonight Show Starring Johnny Carson*. If I could just stay awake through the late news, I knew I'd be good for Johnny's ninety-minute show, which ended at 1:00 a.m. Watching Johnny was cool for a young man in junior high school.

A DVD of Johnny's early network TV work includes his first appearance on Jack's show, in 1955. It's clear from the video that Jack liked the young Nebraskan almost as much as the boyish star-to-be admired and appreciated his idol. Jack previews his young guest's appearance by telling the audience, "This fellow has everything it takes to be a success." Johnny takes the stage at CBS Television City clearly in awe of his new friend. The two comedians work through a routine where Jack invites Johnny to critique his style. Referring to Jack's pauses, Johnny takes his shot: "It's okay to be slow, but you seem to be a lazy Perry Como."

Johnny appeared on Jack's show again in October of 1963, about a year after taking over the *Tonight Show*. Their mutual respect was intact, but the stars' paths were crossing: Johnny on his way up to superstardom, Jack moving into the background.

Johnny did a couple of cameos on various Jack Benny specials in the late '60s and early '70s. Benny's influence is seen in Johnny's work throughout the run of the *Tonight Show*. The Benny program practically invented the running gag technique, using scenarios established early in the broadcast later in the show. This technique creates laughs with seemingly little effort. Of course, any writer would be correct in pointing out that a successful running gag didn't happen through blind luck but as the result of careful planning and timing. The running gag was a common device used by Johnny during his reign as king of late night TV.

Jack Benny was a guest on Johnny's show fourteen times from 1970 until Jack's death in 1974. A clip from a 1974 appearance is part of the *Tonight Show Collection* DVD set. Audio from a 1972 appearance can be found on a double-LP set celebrating the Carson show's twentieth anniversary. In both appearances, Johnny was ever the gentleman in welcoming his mentor and acknowledging a very distinguished career. Jack admired his protégé, especially Johnny's skill at handling the ninety-minute format of the *Tonight Show* without a script.

But even when Jack wasn't on the show, his influence was apparent in Johnny's comic timing and in the way the show was presented. The addition in 1971 of Jack's former producer, Fred de Cordova, as producer of the *Tonight Show*, cemented the influence. De Cordova understood the concept of "host as star" and made every effort to be sure the attention was focused on Johnny. This same technique was used on the Benny TV program to capture Jack's takes. On the *Tonight Show*, a camera stayed glued on Johnny to pick up his takes for the home audience.

Just as Jack had his cast of players, Johnny had his own cadre of characters with their idiosyncrasies: Ed and his drinking, Doc and his wild clothes, Tommy the square, Fred and his advanced age. Often, all Johnny had to do was make reference to one of his supporting players and he'd get an automatic laugh in much the same way Jack motivated his audience with references to Don Wilson's weight, Dennis Day's naivety, Phil Harris's vanity, Frank Remley's drinking, or his own stinginess.

Johnny kept Jack's cheapskate persona intact during his *Tonight Show* appearances. In his monologue on a night when Jack was a guest, Johnny said that up until that very afternoon Jack had the first dollar he'd ever earned, but he spent it for bus fare to the studio. Jack responded with classic Benny timing: "That story about using my first dollar for bus fare, that's not true. The fare was a dollar and a quarter." Two masters of the running gag set up and delivered the comedy effectively.

Over the years, Johnny's conversations with Jack helped us learn how much Jack truly loved the violin ("I would give up ever getting a laugh if I could have been a concert violinist"), on why it was important that he practice the violin every day ("You have to practice, even to sound lousy"), and on the shift from being Johnny's idol to Johnny becoming Jack's idol ("I can tell you now that I liked it a hell of a lot better the other way around").

When Jack passed away in December of 1974, Johnny was on vacation. Upon his return to the *Tonight Show* on December 31, Johnny opened the show without a monologue at center stage. For the first time since the show's start in 1963, Johnny walked out to the applause, and then strode directly to his desk. He delivered a tribute to Jack that included a long excerpt of Jack's final appearance on the *Tonight Show* from August 21 of that year.

On February 16, 1978, Johnny welcomed Jack's widow, Mary Livingstone, to his show. She had written a biography of Jack with Hillard Marks and Marcia Borie. Due to stage fright, Mary had left the limelight in the 1950s. But in the relaxed atmosphere of Studio One at NBC's Burbank home base, she recalled the touching story about the arrangement Jack had made to have a single rose delivered to her every day after his death. Johnny took the opportunity to play a portion of a presentation he had made years earlier for a college radio/communications class on the effective use of the running gag as a comedic technique. The tape he played included an excerpt from a Jack Benny radio program.

Jack's manager, Irving Fein, who wrote the first biography of Jack in 1976, quotes Johnny paying homage to Jack's use of the running gag, calling it "…a fine example of comedy and fine comedy writing, especially in the way Jack and his writers played a running gag all the way through the program and made it pay off at the end." Johnny's affection for his comedy mentor is apparent on the dust jacket of the Mary Livingstone book: "Without question, Jack and his show were the most tremendous influences on my development, on what I tried to do, on what I've become. The man was what he was. He was a man with no pretensions at all. Jack was a very special person in my life, in so many lives."

Johnny joined Bob Hope and George Burns in a 1982 NBC tribute to Jack. The show featured tape clips almost exclusively from Benny's later work on the NBC specials. For all its good intentions, the show would have been better with a variety of clips from the radio era as well as the 1950s CBS TV work.

Johnny was interviewed in a well-executed PBS documentary on Jack done in the early 1990s, hosted by Tommy Smothers. On the program Johnny explained that Jack's writers "never wrote jokes" but instead created situations suited for the personalities of Jack and his supporting cast to get the most laughs.

Unlike Jack, who continued to work until pancreatic cancer stopped him in 1974, Johnny left the airwaves thirteen years before his death. After his retirement, Johnny avoided television for the most part. He did appear on a Bob Hope tribute show and made a handful of cameos on *The Late Show with David Letterman.*

Johnny's relationship with Letterman was similar to Jack's with Johnny. When Johnny died on January 23, 2005, Letterman's show was on a one-week hiatus. Letterman's first show upon his return featured a tribute with Johnny's producer and close friend Peter LaSally. The show began with a monologue the viewer later learned was written by Johnny. (For much of 2004, Johnny had faxed jokes for Letterman to use in his *Late Show* monologues.) The Letterman tribute ended with the reuniting of Doc Severinsen, Tommy Newsom, and drummer Ed Shaunessy playing Johnny's favorite song "Here Comes that Rainy Day." Carson fans recalled his duet with Bette Midler on the next-to-last *Tonight Show* in May, 1992.

Johnny Carson lost a dear friend in 1974, but he never forgot that friend. He continued employing techniques learned from his long association with Jack Benny through the end of his time on the *Tonight Show.* Even Johnny's departure from the limelight may have been inspired by Jack. Johnny supposedly once said that he'd rather leave show business too soon than too late, the implication being that stars like Jack and Bob Hope may have stayed past their prime. When questioned about the timing of his retirement, Johnny said, "I'm getting out while I'm on top of my game."

Fans of Jack Benny and Johnny Carson were the beneficiaries of years of great entertainment. Theirs was a relationship based in love, respect, and sincerity. These traits can't be faked. We saw the real thing with Jack. And we saw the real thing with Johnny. We were lucky to have been there to see it.

# From the Cradle to the Grave: The Births and Deaths of the Principal Characters of *The Jack Benny Program*

## by Ron Sayles and Michael Leannah

The birth of a son to Meyer and Emma Kubelsky on Valentine's Day, 1894 occurred without fanfare and made not a ripple in the news of the day. When that baby, Benjamin Kubelsky, later known as Jack Benny, died on December 26, 1974, the world mourned.

"Cancer Kills Comedy King Jack Benny."

"Jack Benny Dies of Cancer in Beverly Hills."

"Jack Benny Is Dead, Comedian was 80."

*Newsweek*'s headline stated a simple and poignant "Good Night, Folks."

Grover Cleveland was president at the time of Benny's birth, in charge of a country half its current age. Still, you don't have to be very old—just a little over 40—to remember Jack Benny performing—on radio, in the movies, on TV, or on the stage. Time moves in mysterious ways.

With this in mind, let's take a peek at what was in the news at the times of birth and death of Jack Benny and the members of his cast.

In 1894 a yearly subscription to the *New York Times* cost a mere $8. At the newsstand, the paper sold for three cents, five for the Sunday edition. On the day Jack Benny was born, February 14, 1894, the main story on the front page carried the headline, "White Mantle on the City; Fourteen Inches of Snow Fell in a Very Few Hours." The blizzard, mixing itself with "fierce squalls of sleet," was a boon to the unemployed, for Commissioner Andrews put out a call for help in clearing the snow. Drivers caught in the storm steered and stumbled their teams through the drifts. The storm caused the three-masted schooner *Minnie Rowan*, with coal bound for Boston, to be stranded near Third Cliff. High seas prevented rescue efforts from reaching the crew.

With weather like that raging outside, imagine the reader's reverie upon turning the page and finding the travel advertisement promoting Jamaica, "the most picturesque and health-giving resort in the world." For $5 a day, you could board the *S.S. Athos* and head for warmer climes. Today, that'll barely get you a gallon of gas.

For a trip to Jamaica you'd need new clothes. At Best & Co. on West 23$^{rd}$ Street, the price range on waists and blouses was 48 cents to $3.75. Deutsch and Company on Fifth Avenue had a wider selection. A silk-lined jacket cost $5.00. Ulsters and coats were reduced from $35 to $10. Then again, Persian coats ran as high as $160 each.

Elsewhere in the paper, an ad claims that "the best Valentine is a bottle of Riker's Expectorant, warranted to prevent pneumonia and cure any cough or cold, bronchitis, croup, and other affection of the throat or lungs." Let's hope Meyer Kubelsky wasn't so easily persuaded and bought his wife something more romantic for Valentine's Day than a bottle of cough medicine.

Had you been a New York relative of the Kubelskys and wanted to visit them after Jack's birth, the Pennsylvania Railroad provided a train from New York to Chicago. The Chicago and St. Louis Express, with Pullman sleeping and dining cars, left New York every day at 2:00 p.m., arriving in Chicago 27 hours later.

In 1941 Jack Benny starred in the movie *Charley's Aunt.* On the day of his birth, the stage production of *Charley's Aunt* was playing at the Standard Theater in New York City.

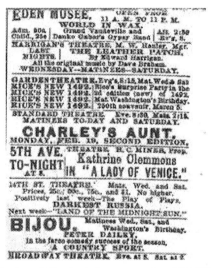

Notice for production of *Charley's Aunt,* stage play. 1894 (*New York Times*)

Jack Benny died of pancreatic cancer at the age of 39 (who said he was 80?) the day after Christmas in 1974, his wife and daughter at his side. Among those visiting Benny on his last day were Frank Sinatra, Bob Hope, Danny Kaye, and Benny's friend of 50 years, George Burns. Pallbearers at the funeral included Irving Fein, Mervyn LeRoy, Hilliard Marks, Gregory Peck, Frank Sinatra, Milton Berle, Billy Wilder, and Fred de Cordova. Honorary pallbearers included Don Wilson, Phil Harris, Eddie Anderson, Dennis Day, Mel Blanc, Benny Rubin, James Stewart, Johnny Carson, George Jessel, Isaac Stern, and William S. Paley.

Don Wilson came into the world on September 1, 1900 in Denver, Colorado. On that date, the front page of the *New York Times* carried a list of populations of U.S. cities. New York was the largest at 3,437,202 (today it weighs in at eight million-plus), followed by Chicago (1,698,575) and Philadelphia (1,293,697).

These were the only cities in the United States with more than a million people. Today, there are more than 25 metropolitan areas with an excess of *two* million people.

The city with the fourth largest population at the turn of the 20$^{th}$ century was St. Louis at 575,238, followed by Boston, Baltimore, Cleveland, Buffalo, San Francisco, Cincinnati, Pittsburgh, New Orleans, Detroit, Milwaukee, Washington, D.C., Newark, Jersey City, Louisville, and Minneapolis. After those came cities with fewer than 200,000 people, including Indianapolis, Kansas City, and Denver. Last on the list, but still the 34$^{th}$ largest city in the country, was Pawtucket, Rhode Island (39,281). Anybody want to take the time to count all the cities with that many people today?

Los Angeles, today's second-biggest U. S. city, wasn't on the list, though its population of 102,000 would have ranked it just below Omaha, in 29$^{th}$ place. Did *The New York Times* not consider L.A. a part of the United States? Was its exclusion from the list a snub of some kind? San Francisco made the cut, but you won't find Houston (78,000 in 1900), Dallas (42,000), or, for that matter, San Diego (18,000) and Phoenix (5,500). All of these are now in the top ten.

Other front page items on the day of Don Wilson's birth included an article underscoring the changes in transportation and horsepower that have occurred since that time. "New Orleans Mules Scarce" reads the headline above a story about wars around the world creating such a demand for mules that New Orleans was left without enough to tend to the cotton crop. Pity the "savvy" entrepreneur who bred mules to meet the demand, only to find Detroit beginning to churn out mechanical vehicles, wiping out the need for mules.

The advertisers showed prescience when, on the date of Don Wilson's birth, they plied wares preventing "weak stomach," which was claimed to be "the cause of all disease. A weak stomach makes impure blood, and this enfeebles the heart, lungs, liver, and kidneys. Strengthen the digestive organs with Hostetter's Stomach Bitters, and your health will improve. Everyone needs it to keep the bowels from becoming clogged. To those who have tried other remedies in vain, this will prove worth its weight in gold." Don Wilson certainly didn't have a weak stomach. Buses supposedly got the worst of collisions with him. Could Hostetter's have been his secret?

Don died of a stroke on April 25, 1982 at his home in Cathedral City, California. He was 81 years old. He had recently appeared in theaters, touring the east coast with Dennis Day in *The Big Broadcast of 1944*. Don was survived by his fourth wife, Lois Corbet, whom he married in 1950.

Wonga Philip Harris (Wonga? Yes, Wonga.) was born, on June 24, 1904, near the small town of Linton, Indiana (not Doo Wah Diddy). Two news items dominated the front page that day: the nomination of Senator Charles W. Fairbanks of Ohio as Theodore Roosevelt's running mate at the Republican convention in Chicago, and a war report from Asia where Russia squared off with Japan. Interestingly, after winning the election Roosevelt invited diplomats from Russia and Japan to his home at Sagamore Hill in Oyster Bay, New York to negotiate the end of the Russo-Japanese War. The negotiations were held near the naval base of Portsmouth, hence the accord was dubbed the "Treaty of Portsmouth." For his efforts, Roosevelt received the Nobel Peace Prize, the first American to win a Nobel Prize in any category.

On Phil Harris's birthday the paper ran a prominent ad for Grape-Nuts, a future sponsor of *The Jack Benny Show*. "Compound Interest comes to life when the body feels the delicious glow of health, vigor, and energy. That certain sense of vigor in the brain and easy poise of the nerves comes when the improper foods are cut out and predigested. It has taken you years to run down. Don't expect one mouthful of this great food to bring you back."

More to Phil's liking, perhaps, would be the cure for "cholera morbus and bowel complaints," a couple of pages later. "'Over 95 cases in every hundred could be avoided,' says a leading specialist, 'if everyone was careful to keep his system toned up with Duffy's Pure Malt Whiskey. It's the most effective germ destroyer known to the medical profession.'" Hey, Remley, go get a bottle of that stuff, will ya? According to the ad, Duffy's Pure Malt Whiskey, at only a dollar a bottle, "aids digestion and assimilation; purifies and enriches the blood; regulates the bowels; quiets the nerves; hardens the muscles; stimulates the heart's action, and builds up and sustains the entire system." Duffy's Whiskey or Grape-Nuts. Take a guess as to what Phil would prefer.

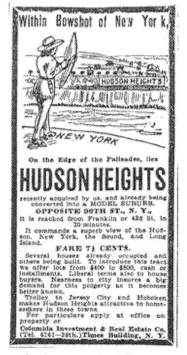

Phil Harris died on August 11, 1995 at the age of 91 at his home in Rancho Mirage, California. He lived the longest of Jack Benny's gang. He was survived by his wife of 54 years, Alice Faye, his daughters, Phyllis and Alice, four grandchildren, and two great-grandchildren.

Mary Livingstone was born Sadye Marks in Seattle, Washington, on Friday, June 23, 1905. On the day of her birth, Grape-Nuts harped again about our health and welfare. Other hawkers included the Columbia Investment & Real Estate Company (the new suburb of Hudson Heights was "within a bowshot of New York." Who were they suggesting gets shot over there?) and the Iron Steamboat Company ("They cannot burn! They cannot sink!" What a *titanic* claim!)

One has to wonder: Who are they shooting at over there in Hudson Heights?
New York Times, June 23, 1905

In the news, we find an account of a train wreck in Ohio involving the Lake Shore Twentieth Century Limited, in which 19 people were killed. The accident was caused by an open switch, possibly turned by a "maniac or someone who had a grievance against the railroad company."

Another story details a plan to use ice and pumps to try to cool the air and improve ventilation in the New York subways. The plan was to go forward with a bacteriologist present, in spite of objections voiced by the City Commissioner, "who said he had been riding in the subway to see if he felt any sickness such as he knew he would feel if the air was bad. He said the air had not made him at all ill." Proof positive!

Mary Livingstone suffered from a heart ailment for a year before dying on June 3, 1983 at the age of 77. She lived alone, except for servants, in Holmby Hills, California. She died in her sleep. Mary was survived by her daughter, Joan, and four grandchildren.

"Negro Murderer Lynched" So read one of the front page stories in *The New York Times* on September 18, 1905, the day Eddie Anderson was born in Oakland, California. The story, in its entirety, is reprinted here. Its matter-of-fact presentation speaks volumes.

"Honea Path, S.C.—About three miles below here, in Abbeville County, this afternoon, Sam and Jim Moore, white, got into a fight with Allen Pendleton and another Negro. Jim Moore was killed by Pendleton.

"Pendleton was captured by a crowd about half a mile below this place, carried back to the scene of the killing, and shot by about a dozen men at 10:25 o'clock to-night."

Two pages later in the same edition, a story carried the headline: "Three Pickaninnies Way From Virginny." The article tells the story of three sisters—12, 10, and 5—coming by railroad to New York in search of their father who moved there for work. A policeman found the children huddled together, sleeping. Newsworthy stuff, but the choice of language used in quoting the oldest girl was offensive and uncalled for. "Why, Sah, we's waiting foh our pa." "Mah name's Virginia and dar is my sis Martha." "Pa done sen' down foh us to come here, foh we's gwine to school." Did anyone really think that the officer in charge painstakingly detailed these exact quotes to reporters at the news conference?

Let's jump ahead now to news on the day Eddie Anderson's obituary appeared. "U.S. High Court Backs Use of Racial Quotas For Voting Districts." "Black Farmer Fights Debt to White Judge." "TV: 'Minstrel Man' Dramatizes Dark Era of Stage History."

These stories reflect the growing awareness of—and a move to correct—racial inequality. Nevertheless, they provide proof that the issues encountered in the newspapers of 1905 weren't entirely put to rest by February 28, 1977, the day Anderson died of heart disease.

Dennis Day, nee Eugene Denis McNulty, was born in the Bronx, New York, on May 21, 1916. Wouldn't you know that on the day of Dennis's birth the newspaper carried a front page story about a Sinn Fein revolt in Dublin? For listeners of Jack Benny's radio show, Dennis personified the Irish people. He was a master of many dialects, but something special happened when he turned on his exaggerated Irish accent or sang any number of favorite Irish songs, from "Danny Boy" to "Clancy Lowered the Boom."

Other stories in the news on the day of Dennis's birth included one detailing the advance of German troops into English-held territories near Verdun. And "New French Aeroplane is Swiftest of All" told of a plane setting a world record for speed. How fast did it fly? 125 mph.

Stomach problems persisted in the world of advertising. "The happy man is the well man. The first step toward good health is freedom from constipation. You owe it to your system to let Pluto soften and flush away all the poisonous matter. Your physician prescribes Pluto Water." Thank goodness, the newspapers have stopped peppering us with ads for cockamamie stomach remedies. They have, haven't they?

The sports page on May 21, 1916 featured the familiar names of Ty Cobb and Babe Ruth. Ruth had yet to take the world by storm with his prodigious home run hitting; he was pitching for the Boston Red Sox. There were eight teams in each of the American and the National Leagues. The farthest west (or south) the games were played was St. Louis.

To get to a local game a person might heed the ad promoting the Abbott-Detroit roadster. At $1250, what a deal. But watch out. The ad says, "It is the coming type for those who do not require a large touring car," and "The seating arrangement is cozy, chummy, and convenient." Sounds cramped. "All four passengers face forward," however. Now there's an innovation.

Dennis Day died on June 22, 1988, at the age of 71. Suffering from Lou Gehrig's Disease, he'd undergone brain surgery after a fall at his home in Bel Air, California. He was survived by his wife, Margaret, ten children, and many grandchildren.

Interestingly, in the paper announcing Dennis's death, an ad appeared promoting "mouth-organ virtuoso" Larry Adler, starting a three-week run at a New York theater. Adler frequently appeared on the Benny show during the war years and did shows for the troops with Benny.

Waukegan. Denver. Linton, Indiana. Seattle. Oakland. The Bronx. Such diversity in geographical roots, in cultural backgrounds. The cast members found each other, as if guided by a sacred star. Born in the age of vaudeville, closing out their lives in the age of television, there for the entire run of radio. How fortunate for those of us who love them.

Jack Benny died more than thirty years ago. For those still listening to his radio shows, it seems he's never been gone. People listening to his shows a hundred years from now might say the same thing: It seems he's never been gone.

Time does move in mysterious ways.

# Jack Benny Is Dead; Comedian Was 80

LOS ANGELES, Dec. 26 (UPI) —Jack Benny, the master comedian who won America's laughter for 50 years by portraying himself as a violin-playing miser, died today of cancer. He was 80 years old.

Mr. Benny was a household name among entertainers for generations. He was a star in vaudeville, radio, motion pictures and television.

Mr. Benny was taken ill last October. He suffered a dizzy spell in Dallas and came home to Los Angeles for hospital tests. It was said at the time that he had no serious illness.

When not performing, Mr. Benny led a quiet life with a few close friends, among them the comedian, George Burns. His marriage to Mary Livinston was one of the most lasting in Hollywood.

One must admire the obituary writer's ability to be succinct. This notice appeared on the bottom of the front page of the *New York Times* on the day Jack died.
A more detailed account of his life followed in the next edition.

# What're You Laughing At, Mary? The Comic Voice of Mary Livingstone

## by Kathryn Fuller-Seeley

Mary Livingstone was perhaps the least appreciated character on the Jack Benny radio program. Mrs. Jack Benny had a reputation for being an aloof person who won "best-dressed" awards, focused on her Hollywood social life, and chose not to "pal around" with Jack's writers or radio gang. Mary Livingstone, the radio performer, on the other hand, was highly praised by critics and the radio-listening public as a feisty, wisecracking dame with a lilting laugh.

In radio-related publications of the 1930s, Mary was often singled out for tributes. According to an article in a 1934 *Radio Guide*, Mary's banter with Jack was the key to the Benny program's popularity. A 1936 piece in *The Delineator*, "Laughs from the Ladies," argued that Mary and Gracie Allen were radio's two most popular comediennes. Author Harriet Menken characterized Mary's radio persona as "cute," a bit dashing with a dead-pan voice, and considered her a "pleasant girl you'd meet anywhere except in the theatrical profession." Comparing Mary to other leading ladies, Menken placed Fanny Brice's humor as Jewish, Bea Lillie's as sophisticated, and Portland Hoffa's as that of a "dumb Dora." Gracie was judged a combination of brains and nutcase, who, in professional life, was shrewder, smarter, and more intensely focused on her career than Mary. However, Menken rated Mary best overall.

A 1936 feature in *The Delineator* magazine on the prominence of marriage among radio performers claimed that wives were essential to a radio comic's success: "In the comedy field it seems to be the rule that a fellow can't reach the top without the aid in the studio of friend wife. Fred Allen and Jack Benny, the leading funny men, are not much better known than their wives and stooges, Mary Livingstone and Portland Hoffa."

(Kathryn Fuller-Seeley collection)

A popular 1937 recipe collection, *Jack and Mary's Jell-O Recipe Book*, featured Mary and Jack in co-starring roles. They tell such wince-inducing riddles as:

> JACK: I can't guess, Mary! Why is Jell-O like a fellow with two steam yachts?
> MARY: Because it's <u>extra-rich</u>!

> JACK: I'm stumped! Why is Jell-O like a woman taking a package of raisins to Europe?
> MARY: It makes a little fruit go such a <u>long way</u>!

"Listen and laugh with Jack Benny and Mary Livingstone," readers were instructed, "with Don Wilson and the Jell-O Orchestra on the air for Jell-O every Sunday night."

(Kathryn Fuller-Seeley collection)

To fully understand Mary Livingstone's character, it needs to be examined in the context of 1930s society. The Great Depression brought tremendous unemployment, poverty, and upheaval to American families, which put significant stress on American women. Mary stood out as a rare figure: an independent, unmarried working woman with full equality, interacting with Jack's all-male radio gang.

Her character balanced several contradictions. It evolved from a dizzy girl to a smart, tough dame, yet when reading her poems or her letters from home, she was still the unsophisticated kid from Plainfield, New Jersey. She was the single girl who could drool over Robert Taylor or go to dinner with men she'd met on the train to New York, but the audience knew that in reality she was Jack Benny's spouse. And Mary's constant stream of critical barbs aimed at Jack made her a kind of wife-with-serpent's-tongue.

By having Mary's character on the show *not* wed to Jack, she could slip in and out of the role of a wife puncturing her husband's pretensions, earning the most prominent (and last) laughs. She got away with her barbs "scot-free," never punished for being what film scholar Kathleen Rowe calls an "Unruly Woman"—the wisecracking heroine popular in 1930s Hollywood films. Katharine Hepburn, Carole Lombard, Claudette Colbert, and Rosalind Russell starred in screwball comedies, sometimes as ditzy heiresses, but just as often as brainy, adventurous women with independent careers. Most of the Unruly

Women were in movies, not on radio. The Mary Livingstone character was ahead of her time.

Mary Livingstone was born Sadye Marks on June 23, 1905. She married Jack Benny on January 14, 1927. She didn't care for the role of backstage wife, growing more and more jealous of the actresses and chorus girls with whom Jack associated. So when Jack's stage assistant didn't show up one night, Sadye, under the stage name of Marie Marsh, joined Jack as his on-stage "stooge." The audience loved her. Mary always insisted she had no ambition to be an actress, that she was shy and nervous onstage in front of a microphone. She was a reluctant performer who was naturally talented.

Sadye was not in the original cast on Jack's radio program. But again a casting need pressed her into service with the role of Jack's fan club president (a young woman named Mary Livingstone from Plainfield, New Jersey) on August 3, 1932. She later recalled, "When it came time for me to deliver my dialogue, what I did mostly was to laugh—because, by then, I'd had enough sense to get nervous! I didn't go on a second time until three months later. Again, out of nervousness, I laughed. You can imagine my surprise when fan mail started pouring in addressed to 'The Girl Who Laughed, c/o Jack Benny's Canada Dry Show'!" Sadye adopted the character's name as her own and when Jack started his second season in March of 1933, Mary became the first member of what later was called Jack's "gang."

While the Mary Livingstone character contained elements of the "Unruly Woman," her radio persona developed depth and strength over time. Initially, Mary's radio character, like the vaudeville one before it, was what she termed "a dumb girl." Soon after her debut on radio, Jack hired her as his secretary on the show. She took dictation and typed letters for him—with mixed results; she often forgot to put paper in the typewriter. Mary's silly questions reinforced her image as a dizzy dame.

She read letters and took phone calls from her mother back in Plainfield, and expanded the show's continuing focus on situation comedy as she discussed the latest adventures of her family. Papa was intoxicated, unemployed, or both; Mama was a strong-headed and forceful woman; and sister Babe, the pipe-fitter, was always searching for a husband. Various brothers, aunts, uncles, and cousins had accidents, took odd jobs, and did crazy things that were fodder for wry jokes and bad puns.

Aside from her famous laughter, Mary's strength in performance was in how she used her voice to give character to her lines. The way she read her goofy poems and lines of doggerel added a bit of human frailty to her acid wit. The verses were filled with puns and sophomoric wordplay. Jack interspersed comments among the stanzas, questioning her odd rhymes, his criticisms carrying an air of affectionate tolerance. The poems and letters from Mama emphasized Mary's naiveté, in spite of her supposed sophistication.

As the Benny show evolved in the mid-1930s, the character dynamics shifted. Tenor Kenny Baker joined the cast and soon became established as the naïve foil for Benny's barbs. Mary claimed later that "when Kenny came on, the writers made him dumb, too. It didn't take Jack long to discover that two dopes weren't as funny as one. That's when I became Jack's smart-aleck girl friend ..." Mary Livingstone assumed the original Jack Benny persona of 1932, that of the wisecracker. The barbs she began leveling at Jack were less silly and more pointed.

What we most associate with Mary Livingstone today are the clever put-downs and puncturings of Jack's over-inflated ego. At their worst, her comments bordered on shrewish and mean. Witness the famous exchange that, according to Jack, garnered the biggest laugh ever on the show, in which he tries to impress opera star Dorothy Kirsten with his knowledge of music only to have Mary cut in with a stinging "Oh, shut up!"

By 1938, Mary was pouring on the put-downs of Jack, and she never let up. But no matter how sharp and mean Mary was toward Jack, she never left him; she was always there to go on crazy adventures in the Maxwell, to have dinner at his house, to go out for a sandwich after the show. Whenever Jack's character was sick or injured or sad, Mary was the first one to visit. This loyalty allowed the audience to accept Mary's occasional harsh words for Jack. Moreover, they sensed the affection Jack exhibited toward Mary, felt the warmth in his voice when he spoke of her when she was ill and missed a program.

In an era that held marriage in high esteem, and in which women depended upon it for economic stability, Mary portrayed a single female who dated fellow cast members in the earliest shows, talked about her crushes on handsome movie actors, and was chased across military camps by enlisted men during the war. Mary could express an interest in, and a desire for, men. A married woman rarely did that publicly, at least not with her husband standing next to her. These elements, of course, added layers to the humiliation of the Jack Benny character, which was the heart of the program's humor.

Mary had a showstopper laugh. When radio fans heard it, they knew a sharp barb would follow. Her jokes were drawn out, playing on the anticipation. She laughed and waited a beat, until Jack or Phil asked, "What're you laughing at, Mary?" or "What's so funny?" Then Mary let go with the joke, usually a clever put-down deflating Jack's pride in whatever he'd been boasting about.

On the program of February 14, 1937, Jack and Phil welcome the week's guest star, bandleader Ben Bernie. In complimentary fashion, each one greets the other as "Maestro."

> JACK: Say, Ben, come 'ere a minute, let me ask you, man to man ... now he's supposed to be funny, but I can't see that fellow Fred Allen, can you?
> BEN BERNIE: No, I can't.
> PHIL HARRIS: I can't see him either!
> MARY: hahahahahahahaha
> JACK: Mary, what're you laughing at?
> MARY: Three blind maestros.

Of all the characters on *The Jack Benny Program* in the 1930s, Mary was the one who consistently earned the most powerful audience response. In 1937,

Carroll Nye, radio editor for the *Los Angeles Times*, visited the Benny set to discuss the laugh power that each joke in the script received from show writers, Bill Morrow and Ed Beloin. Grades for jokes ranged from Belly Wow to Very Good to Good to Snicker; audience reactions were noted in the script margins for later analysis.

Nye's survey showed that the audience responded best to Mary's jokes. Nye noted that Mary's laugh "grade" was a "Belly Wow-Minus." Jack Benny's jokes, as well as Kenny Baker's, received a grade of "Good-Plus," while Don Wilson earned only a "Snickers," apparently for being too nice to Jack. New cast member Phil Harris's responses rose each time he tangled with Benny. Andy Devine's first appearance garnered a "Belly Wow-Plus," but his grade quickly slipped to a mere "Good."

Mary's "Unruly Woman" was emphasized in her impersonations of sultry femme fatales. Her "Mae West" character, under a wide variety of names, was worked into many skits from 1933 through 1936, always to a favorable audience reaction. Mary put on a low, sultry drawl and a knowing sexual flirtatiousness. In skits she gleefully cuckolded a milquetoast husband, sometimes going so far as to murder him.

Later in the 1930s, Mary's "Mae" voice took on overtones of good friend Barbara Stanwyck. As sultry femme fatales became sexy vixens in early 1940s films, Mary's "Mae" persona continued to be a favorite character.

Still, Mary's role as "independent female" had its limits. For one, she never wanted to claim the role of star with equal billing, on radio or in live stage appearances. It was never "Benny and Livingstone" like Burns and Allen. She, like Portland Hoffa, insisted on remaining part of the ensemble cast that supported the star. In Mary's biography of Jack (co-written by her brother, Hillard Marks) she admitted to a lack of self-confidence as a performer, resulting in a dependence on Jack's direction:

> *If a psychologist had ever examined one of Mary's own radio scripts, he would have come to the same conclusion. By looking at the marginal notations on her pages, he could have seen just how truly dependent she was—or thought she needed to be—on Jack for everything she did and said.*
>
> *"A little louder on the last word," Jack would tell her during rehearsal. Or, "Slow down on that second sentence and wait until I look at you before you speak again, please," he'd say. Dutifully, Mary would write in the margin: "Louder, Mary," or "Slow down. Wait for my look, please" alongside the specific sentences, as if Jack were speaking to her when she read her lines on the air.*

Jack's original scriptwriter, Harry Conn, joked dismissively about Mary in a 1935 interview, calling her "an indifferent comedienne." Mentioning a Mother's Day poem he had created for her to recite, he quipped, "I don't care how I write them, and she doesn't care how she reads them—so between us, we get a laugh." Backhanded compliments like this probably made her happy to see him leave.

(Kathryn Fuller-Seeley collection)

Nevertheless, the poems and tales of the Livingstone family in Plainfield were so popular with listeners that Jack's subsequent writers continued them for the next 20 years. Unlike a string of disconnected jokes, they provided a meaningful continuing relationship between the characters and the audience that critics saw as innovative. A 1939 article in the *Christian Science Monitor* on the rise of "situation humor" noted:

*(Ed) Wynn's stunt of burlesquing operas and famous stories was one of the earliest ancestors of the situation hall tree upon which so much of today's radio humor is hung. Jack Benny has made the situation an integral part of his program. There is the situation of Mary Livingstone's family, with "Papa" refusing to pay the rent one month because he is afraid the landlord will expect it every month. Jack and Mary do not bat separate and insulated jokes back and forth. They unfold them in story form...*

A 1947 *Newsweek* profile of Jack and his cast was one of the last to give Mary her due. After describing Rochester, Phil, Don, and Dennis, the author got around to Mary, "last but not least": "Sadye Marks Benny stepped into the bit role—and stayed on as Mary Livingstone to become almost as famous as her husband. On the air, however, she is just the girl who gets in what is left of Benny's hair."

Mary Livingstone had remained a major component of the show until late in its run. She eventually "semi-retired," recording her radio lines from home and sporadically appearing on the television program.

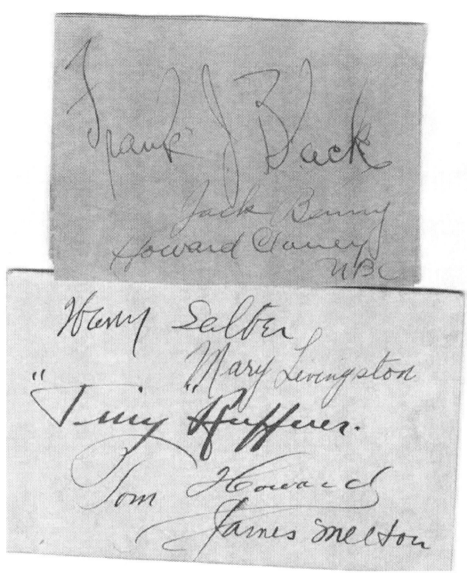

Jack's signature is sandwiched between those of
Frank J. Black (Director of the NBC Symphony and musical director of Benny's show in 1933) and
Howard Claney (NBC announcer associated with Jack Benny and Chevrolet in 1933).
Autograph of Mary Livingstone (spelled differently in the early years) with:
Harry Salter—Orchestra leader on *Stop the Music, Melody Puzzles,* and *Your Hit Parade.*
"Tiny" Ruffner—Announcer on NBC's *Showboat.*
Tom Howard—Regular performer on *It Pays to Be Ignorant.*
James Melton—Metropolitan Opera star and later film star. (from the Steve Thompson collection)

# Mel Blanc:
# Man of a Thousand Voices

## by Marc Reed

A baby let out a wail on May 30, 1908 in San Francisco, announcing the arrival of one of the most beloved voices in recorded history—Melvin Jerome Blank. Did the cry bear a resemblance to the baby's scream heard on the March 15, 1942 *Jell-O Program*, starring Jack Benny? We can assume that it did, but we'll never know; the little baby's cry wasn't recorded. Thank goodness much of what that baby later uttered *was* recorded and is still available today for our enjoyment.

To some, Mel Blanc is remembered for giving voice to Bugs Bunny, Yosemite Sam, Barney Rubble, and countless other characters of the cartoon world. For those who go back a little farther into the history of entertainment, Mel is recalled for the characters he portrayed on radio, particularly on *The Jack Benny Program*. Let's take a look at the life of this "Man of a Thousand Voices."

The Blank family moved to Portland, Oregon, when Mel was six. In elementary school he began telling jokes and stories in different voices, a practice which frequently landed him in trouble. Trouble that sometimes paved the way to success: Mel used the cavernous hallways of his high school to practice a laugh that later became the mocking cry of a mischievous, redheaded cartoon bird. Not everyone appreciated his vocal talents, however. A teacher reprimanded him by making fun of his last name. Shortly thereafter he changed the "k" to "c" and started going by the name of Mel Blanc.

In the 1920s, the major entertainment media were vaudeville and the movies. Mel was attracted to the comedians passing through town, such as W. C. Fields, Milton Berle (known then as "The Wayward Youth"), and a self-effacing comic billed as "Fiddle Funology." Mel had played the violin for eight years, so he caught "Fiddle Funology" at every opportunity. Little did he know that he would one day become the violin instructor of the comedian—Ben K. Benny, known later as Jack Benny.

Mel used his musical abilities to put food on the table, performing on tuba with several dance bands. Portland radio station KGW contacted Mel shortly after his high school graduation in 1927 and asked him to sing on *The Hoot Owls*, a Friday evening program. He moved on to a stint with San Francisco's KGO, and then tried Hollywood. For a year he pounded the pavement, obtaining bit parts in radio—and a wife. Marrying Estelle Rosenbaum, a secretary and part-time singer, in 1933 turned out to be a smart career move. Not only did she co-star with Mel on his first self-produced radio program *Cobwebs and Nuts* on Portland's KGW, but steered him away from becoming an insurance salesman and toward a return to Los Angeles.

After announcing for such programs as *Johnny Murray Talks It Over* and Joe Penner's *The Baker's Broadcast*, Mel decided to try film. Auditioning for Walt Disney himself, Mel was cast for the part of Gideon the Cat in *Pinocchio*. Much to his surprise, when the picture was released, all his dialogue was removed except for one 'hic.' In his autobiography, *That's Not All Folks!*, Mel recalled, "At eight hundred dollars, it undoubtedly remains the most expensive glottal spasm in the annals of motion pictures."

Mel auditioned for Leon Schlesinger Productions, makers of the *Looney Tunes* and *Merrie Melodies* cartoon series, meeting rejection time after time. The casting director died suddenly in 1936, however, giving Mel a new opportunity. Recruited to provide the voice for a drunken bull, Mel was recast to take over the voice of Porky Pig, a bona fide star who had appeared in over a dozen previous cartoons. By the end of the decade Mel was providing voices and sound effects for over 80 cartoons. By the end of his career his voice had been featured in over a thousand cartoons, films, and TV shows.

Mel auditioned for Jack Benny and made a favorable impression; he was given a role on Jack's radio program. He was so seldom used, however, that his presence was hardly noticed. Mel had to wait for the opportunity to flex his vocal muscles.

In his first appearance on Benny's show, on March 12, 1939, Rochester calls to announce that Jack has received a polar bear as a birthday gift. A roar is heard, and Fred Allen is blamed for sending the inappropriate gift. (The roar sounds recorded, not like one of Mel's usual characterizations.) Mel's voice is evident as Carmichael the Polar Bear on the October 29, 1939 show. Jack is hosting a Halloween party at his home. Dennis goes upstairs to see Carmichael, and comes running down with the polar bear growling angrily at his heels. Jack is unable to quiet the bear but a "Shut up!" from Dennis's overbearing mother sends Carmichael into a dead faint.

Jack doesn't learn. On Christmas Eve he's hosting another party. Carmichael and Trudy the Ostrich (Jack had mistakenly bought an ostrich instead of a turkey for Thanksgiving that year) get loose and destroy the house. Benny must have sensed the polar bear gag losing steam; from this point on, Carmichael is referred to, but no longer heard. A blow to Mel's prospects.

Then, on February 25, 1940, Jack, recovering from a skiing accident, receives an operatic telegram complete with "1812 Overture" and razz-berry tuba interludes, courtesy of Mel Blanc. Soon after, Mel provides the horse whinnies in a revival of the "Buck Benny Rides Again" sketch.

For the following two years Mel's talents were scarcely used on Benny's show, but his career received a great boost in January of 1943 when he negotiated a deal to have his name on the credits of *Looney Tunes* and *Merrie Melodies* cartoons. The floodgates opened and calls from agents requesting his services poured in.

Mel appeared on only one Jack Benny program that year, and when the show went on summer hiatus, Mel found a home at Rancho Canova, where he resided for 10 years. *The Judy Canova Show* was a half hour of music and comedy, of which Mel was an integral part. The program gave him an opportunity to test new character voices, many of which he later used on *The Jack Benny Program*, as well as in cartoons.

On the first show of the series he debuted ranchhand Sylvester, whose voice became that of Sylvester the Cat in the cartoon "Life with Feathers," premiering on March 24, 1945. Subsequent shows cast him as Russian singer Smagushniak K. Smagushniak K. Smagushniak, Pedro (the template for the Mexican character on Benny's show ["Sy?" "Si!"] and animation's Speedy Gonzales), Walter the Block Head (a Yosemite Sam-type '49er), and traveling salesman Roscoe W. Wortle.

Mel's impressive work on the Canova show, coupled with a change in Benny's writing team (Sam Perrin, Milt Josefsberg, George Balzer, and John Tackaberry replacing Bill Morrow and Ed Beloin), opened the door to better opportunities on Benny's shows during the 1943-1944 season.

From the Marine Corps Air Station in the Mojave Desert, on November 7, 1943, Mel plays a straight role as Sergeant Gillis. Not to waste his talents, he also provided the sound of a speed plane zooming overhead.

On the Thanksgiving program, Mel takes the role of train station announcer for the first time—and it won't be the last: "Train leaving on Track 12 for Morocco, Tunisia, Egypt, Arabia…and Turkey!"

On December 12, Mel solidified his place in the cast, appearing in the opening and closing segments of the show.

> MEL: Hey, mister, is this the *Gildersleeve* program?
> TICKET-TAKER: No. Tickets, please.

Mel runs down a list of popular programs, such as *The Fitch Bandwagon*, *John's Other Wife*, and finally:

> MEL: Is it *Inner Sanctum*?
> TICKET-TAKER: No, but you're getting warm…It's *The Jack Benny Program*.
> MEL: Ohhhh, *The Jack Benny Program*.
> TICKET-TAKER: Yeah.
> MEL: Who's on it?

After the show:

> TICKET-TAKER: All right, folks, the program's over, this way out, this way out. Hey, buddy, ya glad you went in?
> MEL: Yeah, pretty good show…Say, is Jack Benny really as cheap as he makes out on the radio?
> TICKET-TAKER: Cheap? C'mere bud, let me tell you something. That guy Benny lost his wallet here with a hundred dollars in it…
> MEL: Yeah?
> TICKET-TAKER: I found it a week later, returned it to him and he charged me interest.

Jack prepares for a Christmas party on the December 26, 1943 show. The cast arrives, including the show's five writers. Five? This puzzles Jack. Mel explains (in a voice similar to that of Hugo the Abominable Snowman in the 1961 cartoon

*The Abominable Snow Rabbit)*, "I'm the guy who writes for them...it ain't no picnic, I can tell you that. They beat me and kick me and twist my arm to force witticisms out of me."

Mel's first recurring character, insurance salesman Herman Peabody, made his debut on March 26, 1944 and enjoyed a three-week run. At this time, Mel was appearing on a number of weekly shows, as well as broadcasts via Armed Forces Radio. One of his more popular characters was Sad Sack on *G. I. Journal.* The stuttering, stammering private regularly brought the troops to their knees in laughter.

Mel's popularity with the audience induced Benny's writers to come up with more material for him. The 1944-1945 season was instrumental in cementing Mel's place in radio history. During this era, Mel created his most memorable characters, the ones that imbedded him into the hearts of Jack Benny fans around the world.

On December 3, Mel debuted his rise-to-madness comic ability in a scene in which Jack increasingly frustrates Mel's character, a reporter for *Esquire* magazine. *Esquire* has a file on Jack but they are missing one piece of information—his age. "Thirty-six," says Jack. The reporter tries again later and Jack sticks to his answer. Still later the reporter tries again and Jack angrily tells him, "Thirty-six!"

"Look, Mr. Benny, I've got a job to do and I've got to go back to my editor with the facts. THE FACTS! When I show him this he'll never believe me. I'll be the laughingstock of the office!" His voice escalates to scream-level. "I don't care about myself, but I've got a wife and two children! You can hit me, kick me, beat me, but tell me the truth! How old are you?"

Jack breaks down and tells him, "Thirty-seven."

The reporter leaves in tears.

"I'll try it. That's all I can do. Maybe they'll believe me..."

Mel plays a prominent role in the broadcast of January 7, 1945, arguably one of the funniest programs ever performed on radio. Jack is taking a trip to New York City. When he arrives at the station, he is met with an announcement (voiced by Mel):

"Train leaving on Track 5 for Anaheim, Azusa, and Cuc—amonga. Train leaving on Track 5 for Anaheim, Azusa, and Cuc—amonga."

Jack meets up with Phil and Don.

"Train leaving on Track 5 for Anaheim, Azusa, and Cuc—amonga. Does anyone want to go to Anaheim, Azusa, and Cucamonga?"

The gang checks their tickets. A quivering voice announces:

"Train leaving on Track 5 for Anaheim, Azusa, and Cuc—amonga. Aw, come on, somebody must want to go to Anaheim, Azusa, and Cucamonga."

Jack chats with a racetrack tout. The announcer begins to beg.

"Train leaving on Track 5 for Anaheim, Azusa, and Cuc—amonga. Look. We're not asking much, two of ya or even one of ya, just somebody to keep the engineer company."

Jack goes to the ticket counter. The sarcastic clerk, played wonderfully by Frank Nelson, tells him that all of the trains are booked up.

"Think, man, think," says Jack. "There has to be one train that has room for me."

From the loudspeaker, on the verge of tears:

"Train leaving on Track 5 for Anaheim, Azusa, and Cuc—amonga. Look, there must be 5,000 people in this station. Isn't there somebody? Anybody? Aren't there any volunteers? Please, please, please! I'll get fired if I don't get somebody on the train for Anaheim, Azusa, and Cucamonga!"

Jack gets a ticket and hurries to catch his train.

Sobbing pathetically, the announcer declares:

"Train leaving on Track 5 for Anaheim, Azusa, and Cuc—amonga…has just been cancelled."

Not to let a good gag die, Jack was at the train station again on March 4.

"Train leaving on Track 5 for Anaheim, Azusa, and Cuc—amonga."

Soon after, a woman's voice is heard.

"Train leaving on Track 5 for Anaheim, Azusa, and Cucamonga. My husband is out to lunch."

Minutes later, the woman's voice again:

"Train leaving on Track 5 for Anaheim—"

She is interrupted by Mel:

"Well, I'm back from lunch, honey…Azusa, and Cuc—(hiccup)—amonga."

Later in the 1944-1945 season, Mel Blanc brought to the airwaves such unforgettable characters as Polly the Parrot and Benny's tortured violin teacher, Professor Andre LeBlanc. Mel was established as a valuable part of the program and a star in his own right. He got his own show in 1946, *Mel Blanc's Fix-It Shop*. However, without Benny's team of writers and without Benny's guiding influence, Mel couldn't carry the load. The show lasted but one season.

Between rehearsals and actual broadcasts, during the 1944-1945 season the tireless Mel worked seven days a week. On Mondays he appeared on *The Burns and Allen Show* at the CBS studio at 9:00 p.m., and then trekked to the Mutual Pacific Network at 10:00 p.m. for *Point Sublime*.

Tuesdays found him at NBC for *The Chesterfield Supper Club* with Perry Como at 7:00 and then *Fibber McGee and Molly* at 9:30.

It was Eddie Cantor's *Time to Smile* Wednesdays on NBC at 9:00 p.m., followed by *Ice Box Follies* with Wendell Niles at the ABC studio at 10 o'clock.

*The Abbott & Costello Show* aired Thursdays at 7:30, *Amos 'n' Andy* at 10:00 on Fridays and *The Judy Canova Show* on NBC at 10:00 p.m. Saturdays.

Sundays at 6:30 he jostled parts on *The Great Gildersleeve* at NBC with *Post Toasties Time* starring Fanny Brice & Hanley Stafford at CBS. The Benny program aired on NBC at 7:00. Sometimes that was followed with a part on *Blondie* on CBS at 8:00 p.m.

Throw in the fact that many California-based shows aired twice—three hours early to feed the networks on the East Coast and at the regular time—and you have a schedule that might induce a guy to proclaim, "Sufferin' succotash!"

Mel Blanc's partnership with Jack Benny lasted long after Benny's radio program left the airwaves in 1955 and the lights went out on his television show in 1965. Mel appeared frequently on Jack's TV specials and tributes.

By his ability to capture the essence of a character with just a line or two, Mel Blanc set himself apart from other comedic actors. Some comedians labor through scenes, extending them to a point where the humor seems stiff and stale. Not Mel Blanc. His "bit" parts in radio and roles in short films presented only what was absolutely necessary to convey character, a message, a laugh. Granted, he owed much to the writers, but the written word is only as good as the actor delivering its meaning and purpose.

Mel Blanc was the ultimate voice actor. He rightly deserved Jack Benny's title of "The Man of a Thousand Voices."

Magazine cover, 1960

# Jack Benny: Cartoon Star

## by Derek Tague and Michael J. Hayde

If you were to say that Jack Benny's last starring role for Warner Brothers was the much-maligned *The Horn Blows at Midnight* in 1945, you'd be only half-right. True, Jack did make a cameo appearance as himself in the 1962 WB film version of the musical *Gypsy*, but his last "starring" role for Jack L. Warner and his brothers came three years earlier, in 1959, with the release of *The Mouse That Jack Built*. The only compensation Benny wanted for his participation in this six-minute short was a print of the film itself.

Did we mention the fact that *The Mouse That Jack Built* is a cartoon, depicting Jack, Mary Livingstone, Rochester, and Don Wilson as mice? The film begins with an establishing shot of a typical Beverly Hills residence. In keeping with Jack's fabled vanity, this grand structure is fronted by a sign that informs us it is the home of "Jack Benny, Star of Stage - Screen - Radio - Television"; a smaller sign hangs beneath with the postscript "Also Cartoons."

And what cartoons they were!

Although *Mouse* was the first time Benny involved himself in the production of a Warner Bros. animated film, the studio had made liberal use of his likeness and mannerisms for over two decades. Through the employment of mimicry, caricatures, parodies, and gag appearances, Jack Benny emerged in *Looney Tune*-dom by proxy, in several releases discussed herein.

It's only natural that radio and cinema, the two dominant media of the first half of the twentieth century, found each other in the 1930s and '40s. After all, they matured nearly simultaneously with the advent of both talking pictures and the rise of network radio in the late 1920s. Early radio stars such as Eddie Cantor, the Boswell Sisters, Ed Wynn, and Bing Crosby were frequently depicted in cartoons throughout the early 1930s. The hapless Van Beuren Studios of New York took the era's hottest program, *Amos 'n' Andy*, and transferred it to animation for two theatrical cartoons in 1933; the series might have prospered had it been produced by any other cartoon factory. Luminaries of the ether as diverse as Rudy Vallee, Arthur Tracy, and the comedy team of Colonel Stoopnagle and Budd even found their way into live-action segments interpolated into various *Betty Boop* and *Screen Songs* ("follow the bouncing ball") shorts, courtesy of brothers Max and Dave Fleischer.

Warner Brothers began featuring songs from their films as centerpieces of a cartoon series known as *Merrie Melodies*. One of the earliest entries, *Crosby, Columbo, and Vallee* (1932), concerns an Indian tribe whose female populace prefers the famed radio crooners to flesh-and-blood male Native Americans. The focus of the *Melodies* gradually changed from music to comedy, though Warners' movie songs were still featured; consequently, caricatures of radio comedians such as Joe Penner, Al Pearce, Fred Allen, and the aforementioned

Cantor and Wynn began appearing. They were familiar to movie audiences, and even a mediocre reproduction of their radio traits practically guaranteed big laughs.

By 1936, Jack Benny had been on the air for four seasons. Benny references inevitably began turning up in WB cartoons. One of the earliest comes at the close of Fred (later "Tex") Avery's *Miss Glory*, a color *Merrie Melodies* released on March 7, 1936. Avery, perhaps as important as Walt Disney in terms of influence in the world of animated cartoons, became a master of the visual and verbal pun, breaking the fourth wall, and incorporating pop culture references into his work. The young dynamo had been promoted from a ramshackle bungalow dubbed "Termite Terrace," where he'd established Porky Pig as the star of the black-and-white *Looney Tunes* series. Compared to most of Avery's output, *Miss Glory* is subdued, as its purpose was to showcase the art deco designs of Leadora Congdon, whose work in this cartoon is apparently all of her "glory" that remains for posterity.

Miss Glory is expected at a modest country hotel in the rustic town of Hicksville. After dreaming of a luscious Hollywood star based on Marion Davies (who had starred in the WB feature *Page Miss Glory*, released the previous September), Abner, the hotel's bellhop, finds that his charge is actually more the Shirley Temple type. Abner faints in disbelief into Miss Glory's arms. "Boy, do I slay 'em," the tyke remarks dryly. Then, with a glance toward the theater's orchestra pit, Miss Glory commands, "Play, Don," just as Benny had done countless times to his bandleader Don Bestor.

Laura Leff, president/founder of The International Jack Benny Fan Club, notes that Bestor was Benny's bandleader from April 6, 1934 to July 14, 1935—the entire run of Jack's General Tire series and the first season for Jell-O. "Jack had developed his call to the orchestra leader of 'Play, (name)' as far back as Ted Weems in the 1932 Canada Dry series," Ms. Leff continues. "So it went from 'Play, Ted' to 'Play, Frank' (Black) to 'Play, Don' (Bestor) to 'Play, John' (Green) to 'Play, Phil' (Harris). Jack also used the same call to the singers, as in 'Sing, Kenny' (Baker) or 'Sing, Dennis' (Day). For some reason, the expression 'Play, Don' had some popularity, and it was also quoted by Groucho Marx in *A Night at the Opera*." According to animation historians Jerry Beck and Keith Scott, Bestor had left the Benny program while *Miss Glory* was still in production.

Later that year, Jack made his first WB cartoon "appearance" in what has become one of Avery's most celebrated cartoons, *I Love to Singa*—again a song originally used in a Warner feature film, *The Singing Kid* (1936), and sung by Al Jolson, whose popularity was then on the wane. *I Love to Singa*, released on July 18, 1936, is a seven-minute retelling of Warner Bros./Vitaphone's landmark 1927 release *The Jazz Singer*. In this morality tale pitting artistic self-expression against familial conformity, a pop-singing owlet (voiced by Tommy "Butch" Bond of *Our Gang/Little Rascals* fame) who calls himself "Owl Jolson," seeks his fame on radio station G-O-N-G's amateur showcase program after being banished from the "family tree" by his music professor papa, Dr. Fritz Owl, a "teacher of voice, piano, & violin, but—NO JAZZ!" It's at station G-O-N-G where we first meet "Jack Bunny."

Owl Jolson and Jack Bunny from *I Love to Singa* (1936)

An in-name-only parody of Mr. Benny, this "Bunny" is the cigar-chomping host of *Jack Bunny and His Amatuer* [sic] *Hour.* He serves as the sole judge of talent on his radio show, which is heard at home by a worried Dr. and Mrs. Owl, and Owl Jolson's identical brothers Caruso, Kreisler, and Mendelssohn, all of whom immediately rush to the station in hopes of being reunited with the lost family member. (Interestingly, the cartoon features another Benny reference: when Owl Jolson first emerges from his egg he greets his family with a cheery "Hello, Strenzer!"—the signature line used by "Schlepperman" on the Benny program.)

At first, Jack Bunny approves of Owl Jolson's rendition of the film's title song, after having dispatched all of the previous acts by striking a gong and activating a well-placed trap door. However, the young bird's act hits a panic-stricken sour note when he sees his family staring through the control room window and he reverts to singing a dreadful version of Thomas Moore's ballad "Drink to Me Only with Thine Eyes," the one song Papa Owl approved of. As the act begins to flounder, Jack is about to hit the gong when Papa bursts into the studio to encourage his errant son to "go on and singa..."

Owl Jolson gets his voice back and goes on to win a loving cup trophy, a handshake from "Jackie Bunny," and the approval of his family.

It's hard to gauge whether the real Jack Benny had a vocal coeval in "Jack Bunny"; the character's performance is largely pantomime and his only line of dialogue is "Well, Sonny, what's your name?" Just why Benny/Bunny is hosting an amateur fest is anybody's seven-decade hindsight guess. Radio amateur shows were preponderant in the mid-1930s and Benny at the time may have possessed a greater visibility among moviegoers than did Major Bowes, the leading amateur wrangler of the time, though the Bowes program was number one among radio listeners to Benny's number three. No matter: *I Love to Singa* is fondly remembered by latter-day animation scholars. Though his presence is specious and debatable, *I Love to Singa* was a magnificent launching pad for the animated career of Jack Benny.

Interestingly, Benny, Jolson, and a different owl figure into our next selection. *The Woods Are Full of Cuckoos* was released on December 4, 1937, directed by the underrated New Jersey-born Frank Tashlin, better remembered for his work with Bob Hope, Jayne Mansfield, and Jerry Lewis than for his cartoonography. *Cuckoos* is the type of film which might garner a collective "huh?" from children who chance upon it today on cable-TV's cartoon collections. But for old-time radio fans, it's a wonderful short full of—not cuckoos—but send-ups of contemporaneous radio and movie stars. In *Looney Tunes and Merrie Melodies: A Complete Illustrated Guide to the Warner Bros. Cartoons* (1989), cartoon historians Jerry Beck and Will Friedwald say the characters in *Cuckoos* are depicted "without...giving a hang about what these people look like!" Fortunately, however, the celebrities are labeled by name plates or stage placards. As before, Jack Benny's, er, Bunny's participation is minimal; but since *The Woods Are Full of Cuckoos* splendidly celebrates Benny's medium of radio, the film deserves an investigation.

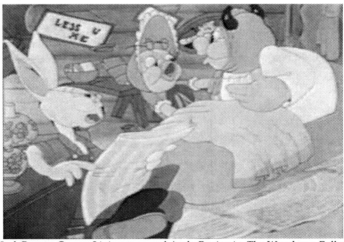

Jack Bunny, Canary Livingstone and Andy Bovine in *The Woods are Full of Cuckoos* (1937)

Radio station K-U-K-U is the home of the *Woodland Community Swing* program, which in 1937 was recognized as a take-off on CBS's sing-along funfest *Community Sing*, presided over by Milton Berle, Wendell Hull, and the Happiness Boys—Billy Jones and Eddie Hare. However, before Milton Squirrel, Wendell Howl (a cardinal), and Billy Goat and Ernie Bear appear, other radio types emerge. Bell-ringing town-crier Alexander Owlcott (Woollcott) introduces the forest forum, then turns the proceedings over to the show's emcee, "the Ol' Maestro" himself—Ben Birdie, whose attempts at wit are criticized by journalist Walter Finchell. Before there was "Fred Allen versus Jack Benny," radio's most famous "feud" took place between Ben Bernie and Walter Winchell. We can be thankful that this forgotten contretemps was immortalized here.

After some shtick from Squirrel and Howl, Goat and Hare lead a sing-along of the film's title song. The Woodland live audience participates, as does a bevy of "celebrity" attendees: a bunny rabbit version of Portland Hoffa ("Portland Hopper"); a red fox depicting Fred Allen; "Eddie Gander"; "Sophie Turkey, Last of the Red Hot Gobblers"; "W.C. Fieldmouse"; "Fats Swallow"; "Dick Fowl" (Powell); "Deanna Terrapin" (Durbin); "Irving S. Frog" (Irvin S. Cobb); bear cub "Fred MacFurry"; "Bing Crowsby"; "Al Goatson, the Singing Kid"; "Ruby Squealer" (Keeler); "Lanny Hoss" (Ross); and operatic divas "Grace Moose" (Moore) and "Lily Swans" (Pons).

After the song, Ben Birdie presents more radio stars—actor "Raven MacQuandrie" (Haven MacQuarrie); "Joe Penguin" (Penner); singing donkey "Moutha Bray" (Martha Raye); and cooking instructor "Tizzie Fish" ("Tizzie Lish," a character on *Al Pearce and His Gang*)—before turning the hosting duties over to gossip reporter "Louella Possums" of the "Hollowood Hotel," who introduces the cartoon's concluding segment, a dramatic scene from the upcoming "Warmer Brothers" picture "The Prodigal's Return," starring "Jack Bunny," "Canary Livingstone," and "Andy Bovine."

The "Jack Bunny" heard here sounds like the genuine article, thanks to the vocal prowess of future *Honeymooners* announcer/*Today Show* reporter Jack Lescoulie. The impersonations of Mary Livingstone and Andy Devine also ring true. However, the gang's scene lasts all of six seconds. Bunny and Canary play doting parents rocking the cradle of their baby son, a giant-sized Bovine who literally knocks his parents for a loop with the gale force of his bellowing "HOWDY, MAW! HI, PAW!" Upon completion of this teaser, Possums hands the program back to Owlcott, who delivers the "good nights."

It's a shame that Benny, Livingstone, and Devine were not fully exploited for *The Woods Are Full of Cuckoos*. Jack and company have demonstrated more staying power than, say, the Happiness Boys; with more Benny, this charming cartoon would seem less dated today. Andy Devine knock-offs continued to appear in WB cartoons, most notably "Friz" Freleng's *My Little Buckeroo* (1938), but more in the context of his Western pictures than of being Benny's sidekick.

If Benny fans come away disappointed in the under-utilization of their fearless leader to this point, the next film may compensate for any slights, real or imagined. Jack finds himself playing opposite one of Termite Terrace's biggest stars in a script by WB stalwart Dave Monahan.

Jack Lescoulie returns as Benny's voice in the persona of Casper Caveman, the antagonist in Daffy Duck's third Technicolor cartoon, *Daffy Duck and the Dinosaur*. Originally released on April 22, 1939 and directed by Charles M. "Chuck" Jones, this *Merrie Melodie* is set in the Stone Age, where Casper and his pet dinosaur Fido set out in search of breakfast. "Yum-yummy! My favorite vegetable: duck!" says Casper, attempting to bean his prey with a stone from a slingshot. However, Daffy—not yet the anxiety-ridden, accident-prone fowl of Jones's later work—gets the better of his stalker at every turn.

Daffy's ultimate plan to rid himself of this Neanderthal nimrod involves luring Casper to "the biggest, most luscious duck you've ever tasted." Along the way, the Caveman and his "hunter's helper" pass several billboards egging him on, including one that takes a swipe at Benny's future sponsor: "With Cavemen, it's Duckies 2 to 1!" The "duckie" is actually a fifty-foot-high balloon. Daffy hands Casper a dagger, the caveman lunges. The explosion sends Daffy, Fido, and Casper on their way to the pearly gates. As their clouds drift heavenward, Daffy remarks, "You know, maybe that wasn't such a hot idea after all!" But Casper gets the last word with Benny's signature sign-off: "Goodnight, folks!"

Casper Caveman and Fido in *Daffy Duck and the Dinosaur* (1939)

Other than the voice, there's not much of Benny in Casper—certainly not in the way he walks. He's not a likeable character either, snapping at his beleaguered dinosaur or griping to the audience about his plight. "Well, I'll bet you're cranky before breakfast, too!" he tells us, but with none of the comic timing that the genuine Benny would have brought to the line. Laura Leff points out that Benny's radio character "is almost never completely in the 'unlikable' or 'villain' classification, as opposed to the caveman." Then again, we're supposed to be rooting for Daffy. This short was one of a brace of Warner cartoons that didn't get its copyright renewed and had lapsed into public domain. As a result, it's the most accessible cartoon with a Jack Benny connection, appearing frequently on VHS tapes sold in discount stores.

April 13, 1940 brought forth *Slap Happy Pappy* and another cameo from "Jack Bunny," his first in a *Looney Tune*. By 1943, all of the Warners' cartoons were in color, erasing the delineation between the glorious Technicolor of the *Merrie Melodies* series and the cruder animation employed for the black-and-white *Looney Tunes*. Prior to 1943, the exceptional supervision of director Robert "Bob" Clampett—and the strength of the writing staff—greatly enhanced stylistic weaknesses evident in WB's monochrome *Looney Tunes*.

Though *Slap Happy Pappy* is a Porky Pig vehicle, WB's first cartoon superstar is barely seen as the thrust of the story picks up on Eddie Cantor's long-standing desire for a baby boy after having sired five girls. Cantor is depicted as a googly-eyed rooster named "Eddie Cackler" who lives on "Porky's Farm." The cartoon ends with Eddie's wife Ida laying an egg emblazoned with "Jr."

Other gags in *Slap Happy Pappy* involve a cow doing an imitation of Bert "The Mad Russian" Gordon's "How do you dooo?" and some fair-to-middlin' Bennyisms. First, a plump hen swallows gravel, thinking it's chicken feed. Her voice turns "gravelly," bringing on an Andy Devine impersonation. "Hiya, Buck," she calls to "Jack Bunny." On this go-round, Bunny is lanky and slender (and clothesless), resembling the crazy rabbit (the one that evolves into a certain "wascally wabbit") Porky met in *Porky's Hare Hunt* (1938).

Jack, working at a conveyor belt painting Easter eggs, introduces himself (voice again supplied by Jack Lescoulie): "Hello again, this is Jack Bunny, folks! You know, one of the Easter bunnies." While pre-painted eggs roll by, Jack diligently scans for rotten eggs, which he smashes with a mallet. "Uh-oh, this looks like a bad one." More eggs pass when Jack exclaims about a fuming egg, "Well! That *is* a bad one!" He reaches for the mallet when a black hatchling emerges, saying in the voice of Rochester: "Hold it, boss! Phew! Mmm-mmm! Heaven can wait!"

As in *The Woods Are Full of Cuckoos*, latter-day radio fans relive not just Eddie Cantor and Jack Benny in *Slap Happy Pappy*, but also enjoy parody appearances by Walter Winchell, Ned Sparks, Kay Kyser, and Bing Crosby.

Until *The Mouse That Jack Built*, nearly two decades later, WB's most extensive Jack Benny take-off was *Malibu Beach Party*, released on September 14, 1940. *Malibu Beach Party* is not shown on television today because negative depictions of minorities are no longer acceptable and in this picture, while every Caucasian star is accurately caricatured, no attempt is made to capture the true likeness of Jack's confidant Eddie "Rochester" Anderson. The Rochester we're given seems to have been cribbed from the model sheet for the truly offensive "African jungle" cartoons Warners produced in the 1930s. The character plays a major part when "Jack" hosts his "Malibu Beach Party," so this Fritz Freleng effort goes largely unseen.

Curiously, though Benny is caricatured in human form, he is once more named "Jack Bunny." Mary keeps her own name (so Spencer Tracy can greet her with "Miss Livingstone, I presume?"), but "Bunny's" servant is called "Winchester." Benny's tightfistedness is addressed when the invitation to his beach party includes a coupon that, along with 50 cents, "entitles the bearer to a free 25-cent blue plate lunch." "Winchester" is shown adding liquor to the mixed drinks with an eye-dropper. Again Jack Lescoulie convincingly impersonates Benny, while the remaining stars are a hit-or-miss affair. (Mary and Rochester are fine, but whoever provided Andy Devine's "Hiya, Buck!" was lacking in testosterone.)

In retrospect, it's proper that Jack Benny takes center stage in *Malibu Beach Party*, as most of its laughs are cheap. After the nod to Tracy's role in 1939's *Stanley and Livingstone*, an elderly Robert Donat exits the party, with Mary calling, "Goodbye, Mr. Chips!" Along with boats and yachts, there are Rafts for sale, a coin-flipping George among them. Clark Gable floats in the water, his ears serving as paddles, and Greta Garbo needs no surf board to ride a wave; her ample shoes are up to the task.

Jack offers some entertainment. First, "Pill Harris and His Corn-fed Cuties" play a waltz as Fred Astaire and Ginger Rogers do a straight dance (which appears to have been rotoscoped from the closing scene of 1934's *The Gay Divorcee*). Next, Deanna Durbin serenades the guests with the operatic waltz "Carissima." Even grouchy Ned Sparks can't hold back a smile. Finally, Bunny grandly announces the "feature attraction of this afternoon, an artist of rare ability and fine technique"—himself. Alas, the applause sign Jack is holding yields only silence, so Winchester operates a clapping device. "I will play, in answer to numerous requests, 'Traumerei.'" With a performance that clearly must have set composer Robert Schumann to grave-spinning, Bunny plays, while his annoyed guests desert the party. Poor Winchester tries to sneak out, unsuccessfully. "Someone's going to listen to this," Bunny exclaims, literally sitting on his servant. Jack then inquires, "Isn't this number beautiful, Winchester?" "Under the circumstances, yes," replies the offensively drawn Rochester wannabe.

In Rochester's favor is the way he quickly became, within the animated canon of Warner Brothers, America's most impersonated African-American. Until Anderson's emergence, that dubious distinction was held by comedian Lincoln Perry's slow-witted film character "Stepin Fetchit." One can hear Rochesterisms & vocal knock-offs in such films as *Patient Porky* (1940), *Eatin' on the Cuff -or- The Moth Who Came to Dinner* (1942), the wartime spoof *The Ducktators* (1942), *Porky Pig's Feat* (1943), *Coal Black and de Sebben Dwarfs* (1943), *Slightly Daffy* (1944), *Goldilocks and the Jivin' Bears* (1944), *From Hand to Mouse* (1944), *I Taw a Putty Tat* (1948), and *Curtain Razor* (1949).

In *That's Enough, Folks: Black Images in Animated Cartoons, 1900-1960* (1998), author Henry T. Sampson writes: "Sight gags are an essential element of animated cartoons. One frequently used sight gag consisted of a sudden explosion that instantly transforms the face of the main character to a blackface racial stereotype…" On this subject, Sampson also writes: "The transformed character also spoke in a Negro dialect" and "Eddie 'Rochester' Anderson's voice was frequently imitated because of its instant public recognition." In fact, one of the WB's crew's favorite Rochester lines serves as the wrap-up for "Jack Bunny's" fourth and final appearance.

*Goofy Groceries*, directed by Clampett, and released on March 29, 1941, takes place in a mom-and-pop grocery store. The store is closed and the products (or characters depicted on them) come to life and stage a revue for their own entertainment. The anthropomorphizing of consumer goods is almost as old as commercial animation itself. The earliest cartoons of this type centered on the denizens of billboard ads, beginning with the second-ever *Merrie Melodie*, entitled *Smile, Darn Ya, Smile* (1931), leading up to the color *Billboard Frolics* (1935), featuring cameos by "Eddie Camphor" and "Rub-him-off." Some other "lively" cartoons focus on toys (*Toy Town Hall* [1936]), sheet music (*September in the Rain* [1937]), and department store items (*Little Blabbermouse* [1940]). However, book jackets and magazine covers were the favorites: *I Like Mountain Music* (1933), *Have You Got Any Castles?* (1937), *You're an Education* (1938), and *A Coy Decoy* (1941). *Book Revue* (1946) was a frantic and hysterical Daffy Duck outing, drawing the final curtain on the genre.

But back to *Goofy Groceries*. At one point during the product performance, a brown rabbit emerges from a can of "Br'er Rabbit Molasses" and says, "Hello, folks, this is Jack Bunny!" He sits back to watch the show as introduced by a carnival barking dog from a box of "Barker" dog food. Acts include tomato soup can-can dancers, and "Billy Posie's Aquackade," featuring synchronized swimming by bathing beauty sardines. When a gorilla breaks out of a box of animal crackers and terrorizes the acts, it's "Buck Bunny" to the rescue, as he rides a bottle of horseradish and leads the counterattack. The pseudo-King Kong, however, eventually has the trembling bunny cornered after scaring away "SuperGuy"[1] (from a box of "SuperGuy Soap Flakes"). "Kong" then bodily picks up Jack, using the bunny's ubiquitous cigar to light an ever-so-handy stick of dynamite.

Just as all seems lost, the ape is vanquished by his mother who calls to him "Henry Aldrich" style. "Coming, Mother!" Jack is still holding the sizzling TNT, which explodes and turns him ash-black. Now that he's "black," he affects a Rochester characterization and comments on his sootiness. "My, oh, my! Tattletale gray!"—a catch-phrase used by the makers of Fels-Naptha laundry soap.

---

1 Animation historians Jerry Beck and Will Friedwald contend that, since this cartoon beat Max and Dave Fleischer's *Superman* to theaters by nearly six months, this is the first screen appearance of an animated Man of Steel.

*Goofy Groceries* was Bob Clampett's first directorial foray into the color *Merrie Melodies* after sharpening his teeth on the black-and-white *Looney Tunes*. As with most Clampett cartoons, great gags abound. Jack Lescoulie was called upon to provide the voice for the Jack Benny knock-off, and again it's right on the money. More's the pity we don't hear more of it beyond his salutation. By the time Bunny becomes a heroic cowboy, he exclaims in a generic cowboy voice "Buck Bunny Rides Again!" and when he's about to be dynamited to smithereens, Mel Blanc provides a "Yipe!"

Sad to say, the final gag in *Groceries* had been shamelessly recycled from a 1939 *Looney Tunes* release titled *Jeepers Creepers* (also directed by Clampett). Officer Porky Pig is dispatched to investigate a haunted house. His automobile's exhaust pipe turns a bothersome ghost black and the ghost ends the cartoon with the "tattletale gray" line.

*Meet John Doughboy*, released July 5, 1941, is a B&W *Looney Tune* pretending to be a newsreel about the build-up of our national defense. As with most Warner "spot gag" cartoons, particularly during wartime, the jokes that aren't dated are painful visual puns. Among the former is a take-off on a Pall Mall cigarette campaign: after narrator Robert C. Bruce waxes enthusiastic about a new anti-tank gun, it fails to fire and we soon learn why: the gunners are busy comparing the lengths of their cigarettes. Typical of the visual puns is an "English Spitfire" airplane that expectorates smoke and flame through its "mouth."

One gag, though, has stood the test of time. We behold the Army's "newest weapon: a land destroyer. One hundred times faster and more effective than a tank." Indeed, the destroyer moves so quickly that it's a blur as it demolishes buildings, uproots trees and burrows underground. "Hey! Stop and let us see that machine," cries Bruce. The destroyer screeches to a halt and we see Benny's immortal Maxwell with Jack in the backseat and another badly drawn Rochester at the wheel. "Hello again, folks," says the khaki-clad Benny, in what would be Jack Lescoulie's swan song in the role. Mel Blanc, as usual, handles Rochester: "Hold onto your bridgework, Boss! Here we go again!" Once more, the Maxwell becomes a formidable blur.

In the years following World War II, *The Jack Benny Program* had come of age formula-wise. Benny's success generated familiarity with moviegoers, and WB capitalized on it with the cartoon titles *Bugs Bunny Rides Again* (1947) and *The Leghorn Blows at Midnight* (1950). Benny regulars Bea Benaderet, Sara Berner, Frank Nelson, and Sheldon Leonard occasionally joined the solely credited Mel Blanc to provide cartoon voices at Warners. Familiar Benny catch-phrases such as racetrack tout Sheldon Leonard's "Hey bud, c'mere a minute" and "Anaheim, Azusa, and Cu—camonga" started creeping into the Warners' product.

In 1946, four Warner Bros. cartoons with Benny references were released. First, Bob Clampett's frenetic paean to the emerging post-war "baby boom": *Baby Bottleneck*. Porky and Daffy assist overworked storks in delivering babies, using an assembly-line processing system and rocket-fueled mechanical storks— all to the accompaniment of Raymond Scott's homage to industry, "The

Powerhouse." References are made to Eddie Cantor, Bing Crosby, the Dionne Quintuplets, aviator Jimmy Doolittle, and pioneering radio call-in advice host John J. Anthony. *Bottleneck* offers two celebrity cameos: Jimmy Durante as an inebriated stork, and an inventor dog in the guise of Phil Harris. This ersatz "Phil" approaches Porky with a truculent "Listen, Jackson," and begins to demonstrate his new rocket-fueled jet-pack in hopes of selling Porky on boosting the baby delivery rate. The device, however, explodes, sending the inventor "back to the drawing board." Fortunately, the scene doesn't end with the gunpowder-encrusted dog essaying "Rochester" as described above.

Voice man Mel Blanc definitely has his Benny co-star's brusqueness and vocal inflections down pat, especially in calling Porky "Jackson" and in describing his invention as a "loo-LOO." Though Phil Harris was himself a living cartoon character and ripe for parody, the folks at Termite Terrace underutilized exploiting his likeness. Harris's persona lives on for new generations, however, as it was incorporated into characters Phil himself voiced for Disney, such as Baloo, the Bear, in *The Jungle Book* (1967), O'Malley, the Alley Cat, in *The AristoCats* (1970), and Little John in *Robin Hood* (1973).

In the second Benny-related cartoon of '46, Jack Benny himself makes a cameo appearance. In *Hollywood Daffy*, our favorite duck runs a-fowl (pun intended) of a studio constable with a strong vocal resemblance to one-time Benny show regular Joe Besser. Hollywood references and impersonations abound as the dim-witted cop chases the gate-crashing duck around the "Warmer Brothers Productions" studio lot.

At one point, the cop, in trying to catch Daffy, bumps into Mr. Kubelsky himself. Jack is humming a happy tune while playing a penny arcade-style "claw" machine. He has manipulated the claw to grasp an Academy Award statuette from the machine's prize pit, but loses it when Officer Besser collides with him. (Listeners to Benny's radio show will remember his campaigns to land the Academy Award when one of his films was supposedly eligible.) In what has to be one of the worst Benny impersonations ever, this Jack—who looks more like WB mega-star Edward G. Robinson—sighs, "Darn it, I'll never get one of those Oscars." Mel Blanc, who was more inclined to create new voices than to adapt them from existing stars, does a pitiable impersonation of his boss of the airwaves.

Clampett's penultimate cartoon for the Brothers Warner ends with another Rochester/Mr. Benny reference. *Bacall to Arms*, a titular play on the name of WB's fastest-rising live-action star at the time, borrows many of the movie theater gags evident in Freleng's 1937 offering *She Was an Acrobat's Daughter.* A lecherous wolf attends a showing of the film "To Have—To Have—To Have—To Have—" and ends up interacting with the film's stars "Bogey Go-Cart" and "Laurie Bee Cool" (voiced by Benny utility player Sara Berner).

At the cartoon's finale, the zoot-suited wolf reaches into the screen and picks up a cigarette discarded by Laurie Bee Cool and starts puffing on it. An angered Bogey shoots the wolf and reclaims the cigarette, which ends up being loaded. (Gee, we hope it wasn't a Lucky Strike!) The resultant explosion turns Bogey into a Jolson-in-blackface look-alike, who announces "My, oh my! I can work for Mister Benny now!" A cheap gag. A very dated cartoon. It's just as well that Clampett went uncredited for this film. Having left the studio earlier that year, he fell victim to the WB cartoon studio's practice of depriving departing directors of their on-screen credits, as had happened to Frank Tashlin earlier that year. Fortunately, Clampett redeemed himself with his next and final WB release, *The Big Snooze* (some pundits find a great deal of barbed allegorical irony in this cartoon when Elmer Fudd tears up his contract with "Mr. Warner").

When Clampett and Tashlin left the studio, Arthur Davis and, in turn, Robert McKimson took over the animation units. McKimson had toiled away as a top animator for the studio since day one in 1929. Like the directors before him, McKimson recognized the laugh potential of Benny-inspired jokes.

*The Mouse-merized Cat*, released on October 19, 1946, was the last cartoon to feature "Babbitt and Catstello" (voiced by veteran WB story man Tedd Pierce and Mel Blanc), seen here as mice (they were cats in their introductory short *A Tale of Two Kitties* [1942]; nobody bothered to update the name to "Ratstello" when they became rodents). They live in Fluger's Delicatessen, where the foodstuffs are guarded by a watch-cat. Utilizing the art of mesmerism, Babbitt hypnotizes his chum, then induces him to stand up to the cat in a plot to secure some food. First he decides to have some fun with hypnosis by "transforming" Catstello into various radio stars: a laid-back Bing Crosby, an anorexic-looking Frank Sinatra, a large proboscised Jimmy Durante, and a darker-complected Eddie Anderson.

"Rochester" carries on a phone conversation with "Mr. Benny" explaining that he's stuck up in Harlem at his grandmother's house, while gesturing to "granny" that it's her "fade." "Oh, come now, Boss!" he intones. While Blanc's vocal spin is dead-on, this throwaway gag just about draws the curtain on cheap blackface jokes involving Rochester[2]. Laura Leff notes, "With the takeover of new writers (on the Benny show) in 1943, Rochester's character had evolved significantly from these stereotypes. This is clearly a reference to his pre-1943 character." The bit is usually cut from television airings. Catstello eventually gets the better of his greedy partner *and* the cat by hypnotizing the former into the Lone Ranger and the latter into Silver. Kudos to McKimson and writer Warren Foster for effectively lampooning three popular radio shows in one seven-minute cartoon.

While never approaching the caliber of Avery, Jones, or Clampett, Bob McKimson did prove useful to the WB organization until the cartoon studio's demise in 1969. At first, McKimson's work was raucous and hilarious in the best Warner style; after all, he'd been Clampett's star animator and had Tashlin's unit at his disposal. But with the slashing of budgets at the end of the 1940s (which led to the demise of Arthur Davis's unit), McKimson's output suffered. His

---

2 Sylvester the cat would get the Rochester treatment two years later in the aforementioned *I Taw a Putty Tat*...and, thankfully, that's the end.

cartoons became formulaic and pedestrian—only occasionally livened up by the sheer force of personality within the studio's stable of stars.

Case in point: *What's Up Doc?*, a Bugs Bunny vehicle released on June 17, 1950. Funny on the surface, it doesn't hold up under scrutiny. The film, which shows how Bugs and Elmer Fudd became famous, includes Jack Benny, Eddie Cantor, Bing Crosby, and Al Jolson.

Bugs, lounging poolside, is about to recount his life story to the "Disassociated Press." While describing his youth ("I was a rabbit in a human woild"), his training, and his showbiz "successes," we see Bugs in action as a dancer and Broadway chorus boy. He's given an opportunity to shine on his own, but the acrobatics he employs don't score with his audience. Refusing to return to the chorus, Bugs walks out "until I find the right part," and winds up a derelict in the park, along with four of old-time radio's biggest stars.

Jolson spies Elmer Fudd, "the big vaudeville star" who's searching for a partner. Jolson sings "Mammy" on one knee, Benny (again resembling Edward G. Robinson) fiddles the Kreuzer practice scale, Cantor rolls his eyes and sings "Ain't We Got Fun!" and Crosby croons "You Must Have Been a Beautiful Baby" complete with "boo-boo-boos"—but Fudd isn't impressed. Then he spies the rabbit looking like death warmed over. "Bugs Bunny—why are you hangin' awound with *these* guys? They'll never amount to anything!"

Fudd, a slapstick comic, hires Bugs as a stooge to be squirted with seltzer and plastered with pies. The rabbit tires of this, and when the act reaches New York, he gives Elmer a taste of his own medicine. Fudd responds with a rifle in Bugs's abdomen, which prompts a nervous: "What's up, Doc?" When the audience cheers, he tells Fudd, "I think we've got somethin', Doc." Indeed they do. A Warner Bros. screen test has Bugs singing the Carl Stalling-composed title song (which had been used instrumentally in cartoons for six years, but lyrically for the first time in 1949 on a record entitled *Bugs Bunny in Storyland*) while heaping slapstick indignities upon Fudd. "And today I make my foist picture," says Bugs, concluding the interview. And so he does…as a chorus boy.

The film is intermittently funny—the repetition of the "Oh, we're the boys of the chorus" song (as rendered by Bugs and Benny's house group, The Sportsmen Quartet) is probably the comedic high point—and the story is clearly intended as a parody of the rabbit's remarkable success. But it's a parody made completely at his expense, as every gag undermines the character's reputation as a winner. His dancing skills are hopeless: he becomes dizzy after a ballet pirouette and winded during an Irish jig. Claiming "Ehh, dis will never be a hit," he turns down *Life With Father*, Broadway's longest running non-musical to date. He winds up a chorus boy in all of his Broadway shows. When given his chance to step out in front, the audience greets his effort with a silence so acute that crickets can be heard. Bugs has always been self-confident in the face of adversity, but in this film he's depicted as an utter loser, and an obnoxious one to boot. It's no surprise that in the end, he's again consigned to the chorus. As Chuck Jones would learn five years later with *Rabbit Rampage*, making Bugs the butt of the joke isn't a recipe for success.

Jack Benny's appearance lasts only a few seconds; mercifully, since his part is silent except for the violin, we don't have to endure Blanc's lousy Benny impersonation again. Benny and the other three celebrities are in the cartoon for one reason: so Elmer can tell Bugs that "they'll never amount to anything," a variation of the line Bugs tossed out earlier along with his copy of the *Life With Father* script. All WB directors re-used their favorite gags. One of McKimson's bigger flaws is that he repeated his within the same cartoon.

By the latter half of the 1950s, McKimson had found his niche: moderately funny Bugs Bunny and Foghorn Leghorn cartoons, and hit-or-miss parodies of then-current TV shows. A few, like *The Honey-mousers*, hold up well today, while others, such as *China Jones* ("China Smith") or *Wild, Wild World* ("Wide, Wide World") have lost whatever satiric edge they once had. In a moment of genuine inspiration, McKimson crafted a cartoon based on *The Jack Benny Program*. As with 1956's *The Honey-mousers* (and its two sequels), the characters were depicted as rodents, but unlike the earlier parody, McKimson enlisted the show's actual cast to provide the voices. The film was to be the first of several Benny-themed (and voiced) parodies. No one is alive, however, to validate this claim, which apparently originated with Mel Blanc. The idea was logical, given the length of time the cast had spent in radio, but the plans fell through. Perhaps Mary Livingstone was annoyed that the 'e' was left off her last name in the credits of *The Mouse that Jack Built*, released on April 4, 1959.

After viewing Jack's palatial home, we proceed directly to a mouse hole inside the kitchen. The hole is being watched closely by a black cat wearing earmuffs...because his prey is practicing the violin. We enter the hole as Jack the mouse concludes his piece. "Who's this guy, Isaac Stern?" Jack says with a chuckle as he puts his violin away

He inquires of Rochester, "Where's my new white ja-a-a-cket?" "I'm w-e-a-ring it!" is the mouse servant's reply. "It's Miss Livingstone's birthday and I'm taking her out tonight," Jack says, donning the jacket and tie. "Mmmm-mmm," observes Rochester, "what that tie does for those baby blue eyes!" "They *are* nice, aren't they," agrees Jack, heading for his "Cheese Vault." "I always feel better if I count my cheese before going out for the evening."

Jack sets off a series of booby traps while making his way to the vault. When he opens it, a guard (Mel Blanc) cries, "Halt! Who goes there?" leading to a routine that amused radio audiences for more than a decade:

> JACK: It's me, Ed.
> GUARD: Oh, hello, Mr. Benny. How are things on the outside? We win the war yet?
> JACK: Oh, uhh...yes. Yes, we did.
> GUARD: That's good. What do you think they'll do with the Kaiser?

This prompts a typical Benny "camera look" from the mouse.

Mary arrives to hear Jack complain that someone has been "filching my best gorgonzola." Don Wilson arrives and tries to deliver a commercial. Jack reminds him that "this is a movie." Don exclaims, "I've always wanted to be a movie actor," and proceeds to misquote Shakespeare's *Romeo and Juliet.* "No, Don, no," Jack replies. "Oh, gee," says Don, kicking the doorway as he exits, "you never let me do anything I want to do."

Mary suggests "the Mousecambo" (Mocambo), for her birthday dinner, causing Jack to envision himself as a cleaned-out cash register. This gives the cat an idea. He writes up a flyer and, forming a paper airplane, flies it into the mouse hole. Jack reads the faux advertisement: "The KIT-KAT KLUB—Cheapest Nightclub in Town. Eat Now—Pay Later. Entertainers Admitted Free."

Riding in the Maxwell (for which Mel Blanc was given "voice" credit in the film's opening title cards) driven by Rochester, Jack and Mary head to the "Kit-Kat Klub"—the entrance being the cat's head decorated with a neon sign and awning. "Gee, isn't that clever," says Jack. "It looks just like a real cat." "A little *too* real if you ask me," Mary replies. They enter as the cat unfurls his tongue. "They're rolling out the red carpet for me," notes Jack. Though the cat has somehow installed tables, chairs and a lit candlestick in his mouth, it's clear to Mary that something is very wrong. Jack disagrees and offers to "liven things up" by playing "Tea for Two" on his violin. The cat removes the awning and closes his jaws. "Yipe!" exclaims Jack, realizing the truth at last. "Help! Lemme out of here! Open up!"

We fade to the real Jack Benny, awakening from a nap on his easy chair, crying, "Help!" He realizes it was just "a crazy dream. Imagine, Mary and me as two little mice trapped inside of a cat. And I was playing the violin!" He hears a violin screeching out "Rock-a-bye Baby" and he glances over at his sleeping cat to see the cartoon Jack and Mary mice escape from its mouth. The long-suffering Benny gives a "camera look"—and the film closes.

Everything works in *The Mouse that Jack Built,* and the result is a timeless cartoon. Rochester comes off just as smart and capable as in the best Benny programs; hence, his scenes are not currently censored. Mary Livingstone provides all of the insouciant charm of her radio persona. The only regret a Jack Benny fan might have is that the short film couldn't accommodate Dennis Day or Frank Nelson. Benny is hilarious, and his real-life appearance at the close is the perfect topper. Perhaps it's just as well that a "Jack Benny & Company" animated series never progressed beyond its maiden effort. The cartoon studio was winding down: its best writers departed for the greener pastures of television, its veteran directors were curtailing their activities, and even Bugs Bunny would take early retirement in 1964.

The Warner animation team must have known that they'd reached a pinnacle with this picture. After more than two decades of service, the characters and catch-phrases of *The Jack Benny Program* vanished from Warner Brothers' cartoons, never to return throughout the studio's remaining ten years of existence. Was this the bellwether for the decline to come, the parting gesture that slammed the door shut on the Golden Age of Termite Terrace?

Food for thought; or, as Jack Benny might say, "Hmmmm…."

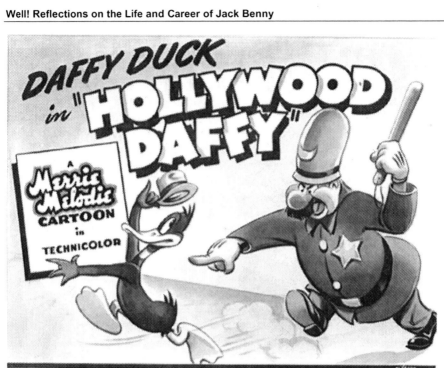

# Jack Benny: Guardian Angel

## by Steve Thompson

It may seem unlikely, but in 1996 Jack Benny returned from heaven for one last comedic episode. It wasn't one of *his* episodes, but one of *Wolff and Byrd, Counselors of the Macabre. Wolff and Byrd* is the award-winning comic book created, written and drawn by Batton Lash for Exhibit A Press. The title characters are attorneys who specialize in cases involving the supernatural. Wolff and Byrd have appeared in a variety of publications since the late 1970s. Their clients have included witches, vampires, swamp monsters, and other things that go bump in the night. In issue 12 of the series, their client was a somewhat inept guardian angel...named Benjamin.

Jack Benny wasn't the original model for the character, according to cartoonist Lash. "If you look closely at the cover preview in *Wolff and Byrd* #11, you'll see the angel had long hair. It was going to be a 'typical'-looking angel. It wasn't until I began to develop the story that I decided to make the angel Jack Benny and his charge Dennis Day. Their characters are so well established; I thought it would be fun to do a tribute. After I'd decided to do the angel a la Jack, I recalled Benny's character in *The Horn Blows at Midnight*. Then I felt I made the right decision to go the Benny route!"

And go the Benny route, he does. Jack is perfectly cast as Benjamin, and Dennis is equally in character as McNulty, borrowing Dennis's real last name for the character. Frank Nelson also appears, as an angel dispatcher doing many of Benny's running gags. Says Lash, "I would have loved to include references to Jack's Maxwell, his vault, banter with Rochester, Don Wilson, and Mary Livingstone, but I had to draw the line somewhere. Benny's character endures over the years because people can relate to the character he developed. That's what I wanted to concentrate on. The Benny trademarks I tossed in were fun to do and, I hope, fun for the reader to recognize. The danger is that the story might become one big in-joke for Benny fans only. I wanted readers to appreciate Jack, certainly, but I also wanted them to enjoy the story and not feel like they were being left out!"

The story deals with Dennis's character being hurt in various minor accidents. An ambulance-chasing lawyer consequently takes the character's guardian angel, Benjamin, to court. Benjamin asks for advice from heavenly dispatcher Frank Nelson.

"Angels leaving on Track five for Anaheim, Azusa, and Cucamonga."

"Gee," says Benjamin, "look at all those guardian angels."

"Yes," says Nelson. "Terrible tragedy down on Earth. People getting hurt, fleeing for their lives."

"Oh," says the angel. "Is it an earthquake? A flood?"

"No, a movie theater was showing a revival of *The Horn Blows at Midnight.*"

In a silent panel worthy of Jack's vaunted timing, Benjamin turns and stares at the reader.

Ultimately, Nelson steers him in the direction of Wolff and Byrd. Alanna Wolff is the senior partner. Far from a typical comic book female, she's tall, businesslike, and wears glasses. Her most striking feature is her white hair, worn in an upswept style that resembles a Spanish conquistador's helmet.

By contrast, Jeff Byrd is a slightly pudgy, normal-looking fellow, albeit with Steve Ditko's goofy Norman Osborn hair from the Spider-Man comics of the 1960s. Though Ditko obviously influenced Lash's art style, Lash is clearly a student of all comic art styles. He utilizes different techniques in both *Wolff and Byrd* and in Bongo Comics' *Radioactive Man* series. He was, in fact, a student of both Harvey Kurtzman (creator of *MAD*) and Will Eisner (*The Spirit*) and their influence abounds in his storytelling in *Wolff and Byrd, Counselors of the Macabre*.

"I love Jack!" says Lash. "I enjoyed his style of comedy as a kid, and even more so as an adult. As a fan, I'm not as feverish as I should be, hunting down tapes of the old Benny radio and TV shows, but I'll always stop what I'm doing when they're re-broadcast. I fondly remember WQXR, New York, broadcasting the Benny show every Sunday at 7 during the mid-'80s. It was a treat."

Lash shows an uncanny ability to adapt a person's style. He deftly blends Benny's physical mannerisms with his classic radio catchphrases from "Yipe!" to "Well!" to "Oh, shut up!" You can almost see Jack turning to face the "camera" for one of his hilarious pauses.

In *Counselors of the Macabre*, Benjamin reveals himself to Dennis because he resents not getting credit for his good deeds. As they talk, he also reveals that he has money left in a vault from before he died. "Oh yeah," says Dennis. "Benjamin told me all kinds of secrets! He even told me how old he was when he died—39! That's why I never asked him how many angels can dance on the head of a pin—he can't count!"

Benjamin's offer to settle the case by giving Dennis beatitudes and spiritual wealth is refused.

"How do you like that?" says the angel. "Here I manage to hide away a little bit of cash just in case that bit about 'you can't take it with you' is wrong…and now some lawyer wants to take it with *him!*"

Dennis's lawyer insists on Benjamin staying away from his client, leading to his amusing attempts to guard over Wolff and Byrd's super secretary, Mavis. The accident-prone "kid" becomes involved in a major traffic accident, landing him and his lawyer in the hospital.

Ultimately, a reconciliation between Benjamin and Dennis takes place. When told by the doctor that his condition is improving, Dennis replies, "I guess I have my lucky stars to thank."

An invisible voice cries, "Now cut that out!!"

When asked if he thought that modern audiences might not understand the humor of *Wolff and Byrd, Counselors of the Macabre,* Lash said, "Not really. Jack Benny's character traits are universal, I think. To the uninitiated, the angel was a cheap, vain bumbler. If the reader was aware of Benny, then it was gravy! I *always* worry that *any* given issue might fall flat! But, again, I thought the foibles of the angel and his charge would resonate, so I didn't think the reader had to be 'in the know.' I was gratified by the response to that issue. By the way, a lot of readers—not necessarily Benny fans—told me how much they enjoyed it on its own merits. It was one of my more popular issues. It completely sold out!"

Jack Benny fans should seek out back issues of *Wolff and Byrd, Counselors of the Macabre* (Issue #12) at their local comic book stores. It's also reprinted in the trade paperback collection *Case Files Volume III,* available on-line or by mail order from Exhibit A Press, 4657 Cajon Way, Dept. 32, San Diego, CA 92115. All

# Timing is Everything

## by Jordan R. Young

The first time I met Jack Benny he was in his underwear. Backstage at the Melodyland Theatre in Anaheim, California, I waited in the hallway outside his dressing room while another fan—a fellow named Ernest Borgnine—offered his congratulations. A few minutes later, I was ushered into the room by pre-arrangement with the theater publicist. Benny's wife, Mary, was sitting on the couch when I entered; Benny appeared momentarily, clad only in his undershirt and shorts, apparently forgetting he had company.

With a sheepish grin, he turned and made a hasty exit, quickly reappearing to greet me in a robe. Appropriately attired to meet his public, he was as gracious and humble as one would hope. If I was imposing on him, he certainly didn't hint at it; he introduced his wife, chatted affably with me for several minutes, and signed a still photo I had brought from a long forgotten film appearance. I smiled all the way home that evening in 1969, having met one of my heroes—a man I admire today perhaps even more than I did then—and having found him to be the genuinely nice guy I imagined he was.

My second meeting with Benny in 1972 was as fleeting as it was unexpected. Woody Allen, in a rare Los Angeles stage appearance, was making perhaps his last attempt at stand-up comedy; in one of the strangest couplings of all time, he turned up on a double bill with Jim Croce, the year before the singer-songwriter's untimely death in a plane crash. I had hoped to meet Allen during the intermission, after Croce's set; instead, I ran into Benny, in the aisle of the theater.

He chatted amiably for a moment but had other matters on his mind. "I have to go see Woody," he said apologetically, as he walked off in search of the comedian's dressing room. I could only imagine the conversation between the veteran entertainer and the seasoned but comparative youngster; I would love to have been a fly on the wall. I have no idea whether Benny offered Allen advice, suggestions, or compliments, but they apparently hit it off—detained by his visitor, Allen was a good 15 to 20 minutes late for his show that afternoon.

I was first introduced to Benny by my friend Eliott, who happily acquainted me with the world of vintage entertainment when we were in elementary school. At the ripe old age of 6, we escaped into the realm of vaudeville, silent movies, and radio, which was then at the tail end of its golden era, and had not yet been dubbed "old-time" radio. We were teased and snubbed by our peers for our hobby; vintage was decidedly uncool in the 1950s.

But my allegiance was undeterred. I lived only five minutes from the schoolyard, and as luck would have it, a Los Angeles television station broadcast reruns of *The George Burns and Gracie Allen Show* and *The Jack Benny Program* back-to-back weekdays from noon to 1:00 p.m. I ran home for lunch every day, devouring mom's hot, delectable meals in between the laughs served up by the masters of comedy.

My most vivid memory of Jack Benny remains his stage appearance in Anaheim, a city made famous by its repeated mention on his program ("Train leaving on Track 5..."). He was booked for a three-night engagement by a pair of showbiz veterans, a couple of ex-vaudeville hoofers named Sammy Lewis and Danny Dare; the duo behind Melodyland Theatre was very successful at luring headliners to the hinterlands of Orange County, 30 miles southwest of Hollywood. Later that week I saw Jimmy Durante on the same stage, accompanied by a pianist and a gaggle of chorus girls.

Unlike the raucous, frenetic Durante, Benny worked quietly and alone. Minus his regular cast of characters to aid and abet his act, the show was all about him. And with Benny, it was of course all about the timing, which was as razor-sharp as ever. Despite the decades of performing in front of radio microphones and television cameras, he never lost his feel for an audience. Unencumbered by the burdensome tools of broadcasting, Benny established and maintained an uncanny rapport with the people that night; he was back in vaudeville, in his element. And it was a capacity crowd.

Melodyland was designed as a theater-in-the-round, and he took full advantage of it, working one side of the auditorium and then another as he moved in a circle. The material that made up the show expanded on his familiar persona. There was virtually nothing new; it was all in the delivery. A few minutes into his stand-up that night, Benny took delight in pointing out the one thing that was new: his suit, and in particular the paisley lining in his jacket. The paisley era—a thankfully short-lived one in the annals of American fashion—was at its height in 1969. I was accustomed to seeing it on my college campus; I was a bit startled to witness Benny sporting it on stage. The man was 75 years old, but he seemed to be thinking: *Gosh darn it, I can be just as hip as the next guy!*

The audience roared as Benny turned this way and that, proudly showing off the lining of the jacket. The paisley was a hit. Minutes later, a late-arriving couple walked down one of the aisles encircling the stage like the spokes of a wheel. Benny interrupted the joke he was telling to show them the paisley lining. He repeated this a few minutes later for another group of latecomers. He didn't want anyone to miss out.

Forty-five minutes into the show, a man walked down the aisle and took a seat. Benny climbed off the stage and sauntered up the aisle—as only Benny could saunter—to the row where the man was sitting. One by one, he excused himself to each of the people sitting in the row, inching over to the new arrival. Finally, he reached the man, and opened his jacket to display the paisley lining.

I laughed so hard I almost fell on the floor. I've seen a lot of comedians work live, and an audience brings out the best in them—Red Skelton was a revelation, much funnier than he ever was on radio, TV, or film. But never, before or since, have I seen a magician working a crowd quite like Jack Benny, and perhaps never have I laughed harder. The bit with the paisley is etched like a diamond in my mind, and it sparkles as I recall it even now.

# Finding Jack Benny in Today's Waukegan

## by Michael Mildredson

Jack Benny's life began in the 19th century. In March of 2006 I spent a Wednesday in his hometown of Waukegan, Illinois, to see if Benny's spirit still lingers there in the 21st century.

It does.

I first visited Waukegan in 1992 after reading *Sunday Nights at Seven*, Jack's unfinished autobiography fleshed out by his daughter Joan and published in 1990. In the opening chapter, Jack tells of practicing the violin while looking down from a second-floor picture window to his father's haberdashery across the street. Jack provided the home address: 224 S. Genesee Street. I set out to find the place.

Genesee is a main street running north-south, parallel to the Lake Michigan shoreline on the east side of the city. I found it easily enough and drove south, scanning addresses. At 224 I pulled over in front of a dilapidated building. The brickwork was intact, but the ground floor windows were boarded up, the roof was sagging, and the porch steps were crumbling and littered with debris.

I got out of my car and gazed up at the large window on the second floor. Jack played his violin in that very spot. The ceiling had fallen in; from where I was standing, I could see the broken plaster and bare lathwork. Nostalgia, wonder, and despair pulled at me.

I turned and met the gaze of several tough-looking characters slouching on the sidewalk across the street. A run-down liquor store stood on the former site of Meyer Kubelsky's haberdashery. I tried to appear unconcerned as I walked north on Genesee. A block and a half from the Kubelsky home the avenue spans a deep ravine. I looked over the side of the bridge and saw a small stream, the water brown and sick-looking. Garbage littered the banks.

Did Jack play down there as a boy, back when the water ran clean? I didn't imagine him performing Huckleberry Finn-like feats, but I did see him poking along in the shadow of an adventurous friend or two. I wanted to think I was walking in his footsteps as I made my way along Genesee Street. I returned to my car, nodded to the sullen men across the street, and left.

When I returned to Waukegan two years later, the building at 224 had been razed. The liquor store eventually came down too. The area's been cleaned up and has a prosperous air now (though if you peer over the side of the bridge today, the water is no cleaner than it was in 1992).

Today what you'll find at 224 S. Genesee is an unmarked plot of grass. If you didn't know what had been there, you'd never guess. Nevertheless, it's where I started my tour of Waukegan in March of 2006. There's an aura there, a breath of history in the wind. It's worth the little bit of trouble it takes to search out the place.

Next on my itinerary was a stop at the Jack Benny statue on the corner of Genesee and Clayton, a half-mile north of Jack's childhood home. Dedicated on June 8, 2002, the statue looks across the intersection to the Genesee Theater. Long neglected, the theater has recently been renovated. In the lobby are photos of Jack's June 25, 1939 premier of *Man About Town.*

Jack Benny Statue, Waukegan, Illinois (photo by Michael Mildredson)

Genesee Theater, Waukegan, Illinois (photo by Michael Mildredson)

Walk a few blocks west of the statue and you'll come upon the YMCA on the site of Central School, which Jack attended as a boy. Not far from there, at 518 Clayton Street, is a modest home that once belonged to the Kubelsky family. I wonder if the current residents fully appreciate the historical significance of their humble abode. I didn't have the nerve to knock on the door and ask.

Use the statue at Genesee and Clayton again as a starting point. A walk south will take you to the site of the Barrison Theater—now gone—at 25 South Genesee, where Jack first performed as a vaudevillian so long ago. A walk farther in that direction will bring you to the aforementioned home across from Meyer Kubelsky's business.

One block east of the statue is the site of the Clayton Hotel, on the southwest corner of Sheridan and Clayton. Here, in friend Julius Sinykin's apartment, Jack and Sadye Marks were married on January 14, 1927. Today it's a parking lot, a stone's throw from the Genesee Theater. Too bad so many of these Benny landmarks had dates with the wrecking ball.

Walk one block north to the corner of Sheridan and Grand and you'll find Walk of the Stars Park, home of memorials to five famous sons of Waukegan: Benny, writer Ray Bradbury, football great Otto Graham, Good Samaritan/athlete Dr. Eugene P. King, and artist Phil Austin. No one can say that the City of Waukegan doesn't honor its honorable citizens.

Time for lunch, and for any self-respecting fan of Jack Benny, that means a Jack Benny sandwich at the Uptown Café at 300 County Street (one block west of Genesee, a half block north of Grand). The place closes at three o'clock so plan for lunch, not supper. The menu describes the sandwich thusly: "Turkey pastrami with Swiss cheese melted between two slices of grilled white bread. Served with lettuce, tomatoes, sliced red onions and our Russian dressing." Jack special-ordered the sandwich at Lindy's Deli in New York City when he performed there. The sandwich was delicious, further evidence of Jack's fine taste and judgment. (I wonder how many smart-alecks have ordered the thing with "Chiss sweeze," and if the staff at the Uptown Café would understand the humor behind that request.)

The Chamber of Commerce provides a pamphlet/map for those seeking the Benny sites described here. The pamphlets are readily available around town—the Uptown Café had them—or can be found at http://www.waukeganweb.net/jackbennytour.html. Using this map, I drove north to find the Jack Benny Center at Bowen Park.

I passed several magnificent century-old mansions as I traveled north on Sheridan Road (in *Sundays at Seven*, Benny called the north side of Waukegan the "fancy" side of town). At the 1900 block I spied the park on my right. Opting for the second entrance, I found myself on Jack Benny Drive, a short street leading to a cluster of buildings. The one at 39 Jack Benny Drive was the Jack Benny Center for the Arts. Built with money donated by Jack, the center housed, among other things, a small theater and the collection of music used by the local symphony.

Jack Benny Drive, Waukegan, Illinois (photo by Michael Mildredson)

Jack Benny Center for the Arts, Waukegan, Illinois (photo by Michael Mildredson)

In the same park, immediately south of the Center for the Arts, stood two old houses converted into a local history museum and library.

A friendly and knowledgeable woman governed over the library. She encouraged me to browse the extensive files on the Kubelsky family. A person would need hours, if not an entire day, to put a serious dent in researching the available information.

The curator of the museum led me upstairs to the Jack Benny display. Jack's trunk from his vaudeville days stood three feet high, four feet long, and three feet across. Written on the trunk in faded lettering was "Salisbury and Benny." Photographs and newspaper articles were on display, but the trunk's the thing that's worth the visit.

As I left the parking lot and steered my way back onto Sheridan Road, I spied a Mobil station across the street from the park. Gas in Illinois was a nickel or dime per gallon less than it was in Wisconsin. Gas in Waukegan, I noticed, was cheaper than it was on the main highway. But the station across from Jack Benny Drive had the least expensive of all, a full nickel cheaper than what I'd seen downtown. Jack would have been pleased.

Next, I traveled west and north to Jack Benny Middle School at 1401 Montesano Avenue, in the heart of an active, prosperous neighborhood. I'd seen photographs of Jack at the dedication in 1966 and now gazed at the site where he stood and said, "This is the proudest moment of my life."

Forty years is a long time in the life of a school and Jack Benny Middle School shows some signs of wear and tear. What goes on within the walls, however, ought to warm the hearts of Benny fans. Students played an active role in raising funds for the Benny Statue and have an overall awareness of the man for whom their school is named. The school administration does an excellent job of keeping Benny's memory alive in the minds of the students; the walls of the hallways carry much Benny-related memorabilia. Wish I could have attended Jack Benny Middle School. Don't you?

The Historical Tour pamphlet lists a nearby church as a point of interest; something called the Jack Benny Theater is supposedly inside. I hiked the entire perimeter, however, and found only locked doors and no sign of anything Benny.

Another stop on the tour is the Congregation Am Echod Cemetery, final resting place of Jack's parents and sister. A fence separates the cemetery, at 3100 W. Grand Avenue, from a different cemetery on the adjacent property to the west. The main road into the Congregation Am Echod Cemetery leads to the Kubelskys, near the back fence. As you gaze down at the headstones, it isn't hard to imagine the spirit of Jack standing next to you paying homage.

Jack's parents' headstone, Congregation Am Echod Cemetery, Waukegan, Illinois
(photo by Michael Mildredson)

I returned downtown and stood again at the base of the statue. The sun had set and most of the stores had closed. A few scruffy individuals moseyed here and there. I wondered if any would hit me up for spare change. I don't always contribute to the coffers of panhandlers, but on this day if one had approached me—and if he sounded just a little bit like John L. C. Sivoney—I had my fifty cents ready.

As with many Midwestern cities these days, signs of struggle abound in Waukegan. Idle factories slowly disintegrate, old warehouses stand empty. Amid the decay, however, are signs of life: new buildings going up, parkland being developed. Downtown bustled on the day I was there. The residents of Waukegan with whom I spoke were outgoing and friendly, pleased with my interest in Benny. They wanted to help me with my research in any way they could.

I met a man downtown who said he remembered Jack Benny coming to Waukegan for a celebration of some kind in the early 1960s. Just a boy then, the man was offered the chance to join his father in a ride to the airport to pick up not only Jack, but Dennis Day and Eddie Anderson as well. There are people in Waukegan today with such lovely memories.

I have stepped into Jack Benny's footprints in the cement outside Grauman's Chinese Theater in Hollywood; have stood on the sidewalk outside his residence on Roxbury Drive in Beverly Hills. Neither experience matched the impact of walking Waukegan. Jack's spirit still lingers there.

If you're a fan of Jack Benny, get yourself to Waukegan. Put on a set of headphones and listen to your favorite show as you stroll past the Genesee Theater, the Jack Benny statue, the site of his childhood home.

Radio listening doesn't get any better than that.

Lucky Strike greeting (Kathryn Fuller-Seeley collection)

# Afterword

Many early radio recordings are gone forever, lost or destroyed, never to be heard again. Due to budget constraints, shows were recorded over. Some were lost to fires or floods before duplications were made. Many were simply thrown in the trash when TV came along; who, for goodness sake, would want transcription disks or reel-to-reel tapes of radio shows after the glorious dawn of TV? The best answer to that question is a grim, Jack Benny-like "Hmmm."

Thankfully, the vast majority of Jack's radio shows remain with us. And much of his movie and TV work is available. How fortunate we are.

In this book, people who knew Benny personally—Kay Linaker, Frank Bresee, Jordan R. Young—confirmed what most of us can only assume: that Jack Benny was a wonder of a man, a rare talent, kind and generous to a fault. We had a hunch. We'd heard about Jack from the likes of George Burns, Jimmy Stewart, Lucille Ball, Gregory Peck, and many others.

One thing is certain: Jack Benny fans the world over are in excellent company.

Jack was a humble man. He'd be embarrassed by the adulation exuding from these pages. If he were here, with great modesty and sincerity he would exclaim: "Now cut that out!"

All right, Mr. Benny.

# Acknowledgements

Michael Leannah sincerely wishes to acknowledge the following people:

David Motley, Director of Public Relations and Marketing, City of Waukegan, Illinois, for help and kindness.

Nicole Fishman, Assistant Principal of Jack Benny Middle School of Waukegan, for the same.

Laura Leff, President of the International Jack Benny Fan Club, for continued help and assistance.

Kim Dalhaimer, Information Services Librarian at the Mead Public Library, Sheboygan, Wisconsin, for research assistance and support.

Jim Strickland, Pat O'Connor, and Ryan Glaeser for invaluable technical support and assistance.

The members of the Milwaukee Area Radio Enthusiasts, for encouragement, support, and friendship.

Ben Ohmart, for patience and guidance.

Jake, Willa, and Sam, for continuous inspiration.

Geralyn Leannah, for her assistance, support, and loving care.

Derek Tague and Michael J. Hayde would like to thank the following people and organizations for their invaluable assistance: Jerry Beck, Rodney Bowcock, Tim Cohea, Laura Leff, Elizabeth McLeod, Keith Scott, Ivan G. Shreve, Jr., Bob Slate, Brendan Spillane, Charlie Summers and the entire gang from "The Old Time Radio Digest" (http://lists.oldradio.net), and Toonzone's "Termite Terrace Trading Post" forum (http://forums.toonzone.net).

Philip Harwood gives special thanks to Laura Leff for use of stills from her collection, and to Professor David Gewirtz of St. Francis College in Brooklyn Heights, New York.

# Recommended Reading

*Jack Benny; An Intimate Biography* by Irving A. Fein. G. P. Putnam's Sons, 1976.

*The Jack Benny Show* by Milt Josefsberg. Arlington House, 1977.

*Jack Benny; A Biography* by Mary Livingstone Benny and Hillard Marks with Marcia Borie. Doubleday & Co., Inc., 1978.

*That's Not All Folks!* by Mel Blanc and Philip Bashe. Warner Books, 1988.

*Sunday Nights at Seven* by Jack Benny and His Daughter Joan. Warner Books, 1990.

*Jack Benny; The Radio and Television Work* by various writers. HarperPerennial, 1991.

*The Laugh Crafters: Comedy Writing in Radio and TV's Golden Age* by Jordan R. Young. Past Times Publishing, 1999.

*Speaking of Radio* by Chuck Schaden. Nostalgia Digest Press, 2003.

*Thirty-nine Forever, Second Edition, Volume I* by Laura Leff. BookSurge, LLC, 2004.

*Thirty-nine Forever, Second Edition, Volume II* by Laura Leff. BookSurge, LLC, 2006.

Website of the International Jack Benny Fan Club: (http://www.jackbenny.org)

Printed in the United States
132360LV00010B/88/A

9 781593 931018